FORGET PRAYERS, BRING CAKE

A SINGLE WOMAN'S GUIDE TO GRIEVING

MERISSA NATHAN GERSON

MANDALA

SAN RAFAEL LOS ANGELES LONDON

"I love you."
"I love you more."
"Alright, I'll take the balance."

Dedicated to my inimitable father, Allan Gerson.
June 19, 1945 – December 1, 2019

CONTENTS

**Grief \ 'grēf **

1. a : deep and poignant distress caused by or as if by bereavement
   b : a cause of such suffering
2. a : trouble, annoyance

Loss

1. a : destruction, ruin
2. a : the act of losing possession: deprivation
   b : the harm or privation resulting from loss or separation

**Mourn·ing | \ 'mȯr-niŋ **

1. a : the act of sorrowing
2. a : an outward sign (such as black clothes or an armband) of grief for a person's death
   b : a period of time during which signs of grief are shown

FOREWORD
BY AUTUMN BROWN

"IT IS YOUR OWN LUSH SELF/ YOU HUNGER FOR."

—Lucille Clifton, *Blessing the Boats,* (eve's version)

I was dragged kicking and screaming into my divorce. I could not accept that my marriage was over, and for months I resisted the reality that my partner of sixteen years had already "left the building." I couldn't accept a future I might face alone, as a single mother of three children. I couldn't accept the present reality that I was already alone and had been for some time. I was trapped in fear-based loops. I lost thirty pounds in the span of three months because I could barely eat without vomiting. I was crying all the time.

I resisted, in every way possible, this ending.

Eventually, I shifted towards acceptance, and this, after some time, allowed for movement. I finally felt that I had completed an internal process.

I look back at that time in my life and see it now as grief.

Divorce taught me that grief is, for the most part, complicated and incomparable, as are the circumstances of our grief. I thought I had faced the worst grief imaginable when I lost my fourth child halfway through my pregnancy and nearly died delivering them. It remains one of the hardest things I have faced in my life.

But it was a pure loss, imbued with the spiritual mystery of the universe. After my child died, I existed in the liminal space between life and death, part of me with them and part of me still very much alive. The clarity of that grief was not the same as the grief of divorce, but it was grief nonetheless.

Finally understanding my divorce as a grief process gave me liberation.

The beauty of the book you are about to read is not simply that it teaches you how to face grief alone, but also that it guides you into the power of aloneness. I was afraid to be alone, afraid to be single. I was afraid that no one else could or would ever hold me. I did not yet understand the truth that this book makes plain: to be alone is an invitation.

Merissa Nathan Gerson offers us a vision of grief that is neither linear nor simplistic, and instead of a formula, she offers ritual. For humans, ritual is sustenance. Ritual is how we integrate the most important experiences of our lives, so that when grief comes for us again (as it always does), we can say, "Yes, I remember you," and when traumatic memories resurface (as they always do), we can say, "Thank you for reminding me that I am alive." The grief work we are invited to do in this book is not only for those who are single: It is for those who understand that we take some of our most important journeys alone. And there is absolutely nothing wrong with that.

February 2021

AUTHOR'S NOTE

"SHE HAD REACHED THE ABANDONED FIELD."
—Kate Chopin, *The Awakening*

When I was twenty-two, I worked the register at a coffeehouse in Washington, DC. The barista I worked with most often was my friend, from Addis Ababa. He schooled me on how to bring in enough tips, and taught me how to honor my food, count my blessings, and be a good waitress. We became close.

One day he didn't look well. I asked him what was wrong, and he told me that his mother in Ethiopia had died that week and that her death was making him physically ill.

"Why?" I asked. I didn't understand yet.

"Because," he told me, "in my country, we scream. In my country, I would yell and let this feeling out of me. I need to scream. I need to wail. But if I wail and scream here, the police are going to come. I cannot release this pain. So I am sick."

We need to wail. We need to scream. And if we can't, we need to find some way to siphon out the pain, because grief is everywhere. It is in our coffee, poured by those who have suffered recent losses. It is on the news, and in the subtexts of our friends' Instagram feeds. Grief is as ever-present as sexuality and it, too, requires a release—an orgasm for mourning, a pouring out of that which is contained in the body, ignored, and not attended to.

We are, as a culture, chronically grief ridden.

The question is how to grieve, how to feel, how to mourn without blasting to smithereens. Most of us don't have a script that allows us to release our grief like the one my friend was taught, and even if we do, we often cannot honor it within new cultural milieus, living within systems of social codes that preclude us from our origin practices. So many of us were never taught how to grieve, who to speak to, what to do, or when to quit. Sure, the Bible says to sow in tears and reap in gladness, but whose priest or rabbi or guru sat them down and slowly explained what grief is, why it must be honored, and how to grieve? Not mine.

With no model, no set of clear instructions as to how to move through the treacheries of loss, I had questions.

What does it mean to mourn properly? How much grief is too much grief? What if you call on your friends but they don't want to comfort you anymore? What is allowed in the process of grieving? Who decides what is allowed? If we are not all following one set of rules, what is appropriate? Is there a wrong way to grieve?

It took me four decades to learn how to grieve. It took me four decades to build practices into my life that allowed me to honor my grief, not just through ecstatic crying, but through caring for my body, for my home, and tending to my feelings.

Grief is a practice.

This book is a map.

This book posits the idea that grief is not to be recovered from, but rather prepared for; it is not predictable in linear stages, but rather a wild storm to ride out, to learn to navigate individually, before the next and the next and the next grief arrives.

Grief is a fact of life.

In these pages you will find ways to decode your own grief scripts, to pave new paths in your everyday life that will offer resilience. Where you see the word *woman*, it signifies those who inhabit this role in their lives: both cis and trans women, femmes, androgynous and non-binary folks, feminine-of-center, and beyond. And where you see the word *we*, it is not meant to signify a common experience of race, class, and religion; every person comes with their own layering of grief, culture, and oppression or lack thereof. *We* refers to the collective—to all of the people on this planet navigating loss, nuances and all.

A reminder: There is pain in these pages. Please tend to yourself as you pore through these words. Listen to your body, slow down, shut the book, do whatever it is you need to do to care for yourself as you navigate.

We need to grieve. We need to get out of our own way. We need to feel the weight of sadness poured over our lives before, during, and after 2020; we need to do so because the joy and pleasure on the other side is the medicine of our times. We need to feel good, to come hard, to dance, and to laugh, because that's the strength that lights the way. Because life is short, grief is bittersweet, and happiness comes from actually leaning, feeling, and falling into our misery.

INTRODUCTION

**"TO BE UNWED AND FEMALE WAS TO SUCCUMB TO AN ILLNESS
WITH ONLY ONE KNOWN CURE: MARRIAGE."**
—Susan Faludi, *Backlash*

When my amazing 103-year-old grandmother passed, I was bereft and sought the care of a local chaplain. This is what she told me: "When my father died, I fell into my husband's arms. He held me. I still need him when the feelings get hard. I don't think it's healthy that you are all alone. How can you possibly grieve this way?"

The message I heard loud and clear in the heteronormative world that shaped me was that the best way to grieve is in the arms of a man. The best way is the married way, of course.

My grief, I devised from our chat, was not only more difficult without a wedded spouse by my side, but it was *wrong.* I started to wonder: What was I supposed to do since I needed to grieve while single? And what about people like my Great Aunt Mildred who lived it up in fox fur coats and moved alone to Cuba? People who weren't the "marrying type," as my grandmother put it. How on earth did Mildred grieve the losses that came her way all those years without that perfect husband to grip her in her grief? Where was the map for solo emotional navigation? What would happen if I needed to cry over a loss, alone?

Were we, the single people, marked with a scarlet *S*?

For much of my twenties, when I was more religious, I prayed for partnership. I really held, year after year, this vision that God, or whoever was in charge of my love life, was going to bring me someone. According to life coaches, TV shows, and spiritual advisors, I was supposed to prepare my emotional interior and "love me" so my soulmate could find me. I tried reprogramming my neurosis, putting sticky notes with positive affirmations around the house, and heralding the power of praise and gratitude. I was given books on finding the perfect partner, drawing in "the one." People suggested twelve-step plans, oils, burning rituals, mantras, all of it. I was told that therapy and self-work would unveil this special someone, that my soul map was going to yield a person, and soon.

To be fair, I only went part way with this "call in a partner" cure because I was more interested in my creative and academic research, the varying projects that gripped me as an individual. More often than not I put partner hunting aside, only occasionally remembering to write out prayers and intentions, "manifesting the one," so to speak.

Still, it seemed if I lived well, and I lived right, that I would magnetically attract a person as a reward. When I turned thirty-three, and this person did not arrive, I felt I had failed. At thirty-four, then thirty-five, then thirty-six I still wondered about marriage. I thought about life paths and karma. Being "alone" became a stigma at thirty-seven. Alone was not normal.

The 1950s' ideal of heterosexual marital bliss was hammered into me in my upper-middle-class DC childhood—religiously, socially, and culturally. The heralded husband idea was something I had to buck up against as I made almost every choice after the age of twenty. Facing and dismantling the binding social constructs derived from old and sexist models that told me I was bad for being single was integral to my ability to fully and deeply grieve the wholly unexpected losses that would come my way. Instead of crying that Tinder wasn't yielding marital bliss, or feeling ashamed that my life didn't echo the lives of 95 percent of the people I knew, joint healthcare and all, I learned to relish my single life.

Yes, even in the storms of grief, even through the greatest loss I've ever known—the death of my father—I relished my single life.

And still, a model for how to grieve while single was hard to come by.

Popular culture encourages burying hard feelings and relishing Botox and perpetual youth—Kylie and Kendall and all. Heteronormative dating shows encourage us to marry anyone for the sake of being married, and death is often depicted as frivolous and inconsequential in films and on the news. Grief and the emotional aftermath of death itself are more often entirely hidden and anesthetized.

How, then, can we locate a model for how to grieve, let alone how to grieve while single?

It took the passing of my father for me to learn about the *moirologist*: the sobber, wailer, or crier—a non-married woman hired for centuries in Egypt, China, South

Africa, and beyond. Her job was to strike the earth, tear at her hair, scream and wail and provoke others to grieve for the dead. Coaxing the sadness from people, she played a valuable social role.

As an American Jewish woman descending from Holocaust survivors, I started to wonder if I had been born grieving. I come from a line of murdered people and survivors. I come from a line of babies, dead. I started to feel the darkest depths of my grief before I realized that I also come from strength, that I was brought into this world with stories of horror beside stories of resilience and survival, joy and perseverance—not just suffering. It was then that I first began to understand what it might mean to be a figure capable of moving the sorrow through the people.

Our contemporary culture has no celebrated category, no financial incentive, no preset parties sanctioned for the woman who makes a life on her own, who lives alone, who cooks alone, who does it all without a partner. If feminism means equality and autonomy, why on earth is there no empowering economic and social system in place, as there is for married couples, to herald and celebrate a woman doing it all on her own?

Maybe this is because single women defy a longstanding social and economic order. An order that hinges on the unification of two families—and their respective bank accounts—for the added purpose of coming together and having sex in order to make heirs bound in legal and religious agreement.

The single woman betrays the patriarchal economic and social order, and for that—and for being an emblem of aloneness, of the horrid possibility of loneliness—people fear her.

And I do believe people fear her, the solitary woman, just as they often fear the griever, an emblem of the suffering we so badly want to forget is coming.

So, let *me* be your wailer. I will sing you a dirge. Let me tear my hair, toss myself towards the open grave, scream with abandon. I am here, for you, to navigate the depths of loss, to lay a path, so your stepping is easier.

This book is the play-by-play guide to how, without a life partner, I miraculously managed to continue living, loving, and celebrating my life. A life that included grieving while single.

Despite the concerns of others, despite the models I was given and the message that I would not be able to navigate loss without a partner, I was able—with the support of friends, mentors, and community—to find wells of love and care in the midst of the greatest loss of my life. I was able to grieve while single—truly, madly, deeply, and beautifully.

This is my story, one of a white American woman coming to terms with her grief, and the systems that dictated its expression. Wherever it echoes with your grief, over any loss under the sun, wherever you glean meaning in the pages to follow, my hope is that my story, as particular as it is, supports you in your grief, however particular it may be. I hope, too, that the tools offered to navigate the inevitability of loss in this one wild life make every step of your path as griever easier and clearer. With or without a husband by your side.

This is the single woman's guide to grieving.

PART I

LIFE BEFORE DEATH

"WHAT IS DEATH, I ASK.
WHAT IS LIFE, YOU ASK."

—Anne Sexton, *The Death Notebooks*

CHAPTER 1

HOME (ALONE): WHAT DO I NEED? HOW DO I EVEN KNOW?

"DO YOU THINK SHE WAS LOSING HER BREATH OR CATCHING IT? I THINK SHE WAS CATCHING IT."

—Selah Saterstrom, *The Pink Institution*

The biggest commitment I ever made was not to a person, but to a house.

In May of 2019, I fell deeply in love with a one-hundred-year-old purple and yellow double shotgun conversion in Mid-City, New Orleans, flanked by loquat, kumquat, lemon and grapefruit trees, jasmine and trumpet flowers. It was love at first sight.

In the midst of tornado warnings and flash floods, my six-foot-four, husky, larger-than-life father, Allan, accompanied me to New Orleans at the drop of a hat to see the property. The house had been lovingly tended for forty-five years by an academic couple who downsized to an apartment a few blocks away.

My father and I became very close in the spring of 2019, mainly because he discovered I was really depressed. For years we fought so much, and now suddenly we were aligned because he wanted to help me figure out another life for myself, because he believed in my future, and in me.

The last thing my father did in this life was help me to set up a home base. We were both a bit desperate for me to find my place in the world.

There were loud emergency weather sirens when we arrived in New Orleans, and all of the cars were parked up on the medians. The car rental agency called us to make sure we moved our rental to higher ground so that it wouldn't float away. I revered the resilience of this post apocalyptic land: nearly every electric line, every store, every restaurant, every home we encountered was a feat of Katrina levee breaks survival.

When the storms subsided, we wandered the neighborhood and city, assessing my choice to move from the silence of the woods of New England to the thick of stormy New Orleans. Meandering through antique stores in the French Quarter, downing ice cream and sno-balls and Frosé to cope with the extreme summer heat, we talked through every angle of my decision: the proximity to City Park, the potential to make new friends, the affordability, the floods—all of it. We ate fried chicken and pecan pie at Dookie Chase, pastrami and eggs at Stein's, hummus and pita at Saba until we were so full, we could hardly walk.

Stuffed to the brim, he helped me figure out the logistics of the finances so I could make this move happen for myself. Helping me to move into a home of my own was suddenly his biggest priority.

I called my father *Aba*, Dad, Daddy, Allan. And he began to call me *balabusta*, a Yiddish word referring to a female head of her own household. A house was a privilege that eluded my father for the earlier portions of his life. Born in Uzbekistan, my father arrived from a German Displaced Persons camp to the US at age five. On arrival at Ellis Island, he moved to temporary immigrant housing before moving to Brooklyn, and then to a multi-family tenement apartment in the Bronx. He was ridiculed for not speaking English as a child, and at times he wore his ration card from his time in the refugee camp around his neck as an adult.

My father helped to set me up for the treacherous year to come, launching me into a life all my own.

It wasn't just the privilege I had to afford a home, or the parental hand holding that helped make this happen. Moving to a new city and buying a home alone also required that I brace myself to defy a norm, to stop holding my breath waiting for someone else to come along and make all my dreams come true.

I was ready.

I took a gamble, a fat leap of faith towards an unknown future, and I moved to New Orleans for a completely fresh start in an unfamiliar city where I had only one or two acquaintances and a thirst for change.

I was breaking script. I was growing up. I said goodbye to my parents—my father very uncharacteristically cried as I drove away—and settled into a house of my own.

It was awful. And amazing. And it grew me a whole new set of wings.

The way moving to a new place tossed me into chaos and unknowns that eventually would be reordered, revealed, and lived, was not so different from the larger grief that was soon to come. Both put me in a period of chaos. Both were profoundly disorienting. Both required that I leave behind loved ones. Both were new worlds, new internal and external landscapes that, yes, I would find myself able to adjust to. And everything that I did to brace myself for the transition of my move was practice, I realized, for bracing for the transitions of other, greater losses.

It was 100 degrees and 100 percent humidity when I arrived in New Orleans in early September, and it would remain so much into October. The AC was broken on arrival. A gas line was erroneously installed. I had mice pooping in my shoes. Carbon monoxide monitors needed fixing, and I had broken gutters.

You know this moment, when everything collapses just as you start to build yourself up.

When I got to New Orleans, I mourned the fairy tale in my head and faced the reality. Formosan termites that looked like millions of tiny gooey aliens were devouring the wood frames of my windows. There was a strange smell under the floor in my room. There were so many animals in the attic, I felt like Dr. Doolittle. This was not the fun ride I expected from my fantasy new beginning. And this was just the tip of the iceberg.

I preempted my own loneliness and sense of overwhelming duties by immediately putting comforting plans in place. Knowing I was navigating all of this alone, I asked people to come and stay with me in the new house, every weekend for the first month. First it was my mother, then my sister, then my brother. I knew that without them— and their help with filling the pantry with kitchen items, like my mom did, or scouting all local coworking cafes and screwing chairs together like my sister did, or Costco runs and de-molding furniture, like my brother did—I wouldn't be able to manage. In particular, I knew that their company would buffer me in my grief and loneliness as I transitioned from my old life to my new one. These plans made it easier in times when I was sure to miss my friends, fear the future, or pity myself.

Like clockwork, a week after my move south, my older sister, Daniela, flew down to New Orleans. I made her a very dusty bed on the floor, and we spent our first Saturday at a yard sale in Algiers Point, Louisiana, a beautiful and quiet area across the Mississippi from the French Quarter, by the levee. Movers were scheduled to arrive that day at my parents' house in DC to pick up my furniture. While my sister looked at antiques, I called my father, who promised he would meet the movers in five minutes, let them in, and Facetime me to make sure they got the right items. With me, he had always been a man of his word.

But when the time came, and passed, I kept calling my dad on repeat, and he didn't answer. I was intermittently phoning the movers, and awkwardly breaking down with them:

"Please, sir, could you bang on the door, like a lot? I am worried something happened to my father."

Suddenly, my dad picked up on Facetime, forty-five long minutes later, beaming an ear-to-ear smile as if the phone had rung for the first, and not the fiftieth, time. "Hi, Merissa!" He was sitting on an armchair in his bedroom, cheery, ankle crossed over leg, a journal nearby. He was having a leisurely Saturday.

"Dad!" I was nearly screaming. "What's going on? The mover is downstairs, I told you!"

"What mover? I have to go to the airport!"

There was no flight that day. He wasn't making any sense.

The following week my brother, David, flew in from Los Angeles. We did house tasks galore, Home Depot and Harold's Plants, gardening, and over-indulgent food hunting—breakfast tacos at Pagoda, fried fish at Marjie's, and caramel-crusted drumsticks at Mopho. We drove to Cafe Du Monde for beignets, sped through a too rowdy Bourbon Street, and by evening went to dinner at Atchafalaya where we Facetimed my parents to share the delight. My mother answered, and beside her was my father, clad in a patterned blue hospital gown, propped up in a hospital bed.

That was the most jarring image of the months to come: the moment that my immortal father became mortal. What. On. Earth. Was. Happening.

The following day, my brother and I wandered around in sweats, like zombies, completely shaken by the possibilities a father in a hospital room implied—and by our father's sudden departure from a perfectly healthy, vibrant life. Over the course of one single week my brilliant poet, photographer, groundbreaking-international-lawyer father was no longer quick-minded. He could no longer stand up without falling over. He could only text with consonant letters.

David quickly flew back to DC to help my mother at home, leaving me in New Orleans. There were lizards literally spilling out of my mailbox, there were flies, spiders, and Palmetto bugs the size of my thumb, and the rain and floods had started to threaten to steal cars from in front of my house. I was alone.

A house and its creepy crawling visitors I could handle on my own. A dying parent was another thing altogether.

This is what I call pre-grief, a therapist might label it "anticipatory grief." But really, it is just grief. I had already begun to lose my father as I knew him. A grief before the loss death would bring, a sub-loss—and for me it was mixing with a greater unknown of a new city. I was adjusting to unknowns on so many fronts, missing my friends terribly, fearing the consequences of my choices, worried the house would never come together into a home. These fears and smaller losses needed tending so that I had the space and the stability for the larger ones to come.

You have permission, even in the throes of the best thing that ever happened to you, to cry about what you are leaving behind, or what horrible bad luck you had this week, or your dying father. Whatever it is you need to mourn, you have my permission.

So we grieve. We grieve the lives we did not make for ourselves, the friends who moved on. We grieve our last apartment, the last president, our dead grandma. We grieve the loss of aesthetics, the end of standards, the death of so many. We grieve racial violence, a system we struggle to permeate and alter, the death of good people for no good reason. We grieve. Empty out. And make space for the next love, the next loss, to fill us, empty us, move us through living this one life.

My dad declined steadily from that day forward. And I was in New Orleans setting up a home so far away from him.

I knew then I needed backup. I knew the tidal wave coming toward me was more powerful than my little kickers. I couldn't make it out of this one alone. I knew there would be bigger grief coming, bouts of loneliness, fear, and an overwhelming sense of having to do it all by myself in a new place. Something about the extreme nature of the situation pushed me down into myself in a different way, a way I hadn't felt before. I trusted what I knew. I acted accordingly. Between moving and a sick parent, I would need to take deeper, more careful, much better care of myself in the months to come. I would need to work harder to identify my needs.

My father was morphing quickly into another character, still with the same essence and wisdom, but his affect, facial expressions, tempo, and humor had all changed. His brain was unwell. With what, we weren't yet sure.

This was the I-live-in-a-fold-between-the-past-and-the-future-and-everything-right-here-is-a-mess-of-tasks-and-chaos grief. This was a grief of anticipation, of waiting, and yet also of real loss. The innocent belief that my father would never die was over, the space of who my father was as stronghold, as permanent overseeing fixture, this was done now, over. I was grieving, and waiting for more grief, enormous grief, to arrive.

When this first tidal wave of grief appears, and you call in the emotional support troops (yes, it's okay to call them in), everyone and their mother is going to think they know what you need. People had so many words for me.

"You need to rest."

"You need to pray."

"You need to work out."

"You need a drink."

But the fact is, I just needed to listen to myself. I already knew what I needed: people to listen, hugs, quiet and caring company, food, fun, and distraction.

I bet if you listen to yourself, you, too, *already know what you need*.

You are your own life partner. You are your best friend. You know how to help a body rest, your body. You know when you need more, or less. No one on earth knows you better than you.

And your body has cues—you just have to listen closely for them. Especially those we are trained to ignore. For instance, when the combination of moving, being lonely, and dealing with medical details was too much, my heart would race. I would have stomach trouble and neck pain. Your body has its own world of signals as well. Maybe shortness of breath? Maybe abdominal pain? Your signals that something is out of balance. Bodies are magic and wise. They know. And when they tell us, and when we listen, the mechanisms built into us work to protect us, even in times of grief.

We are our own planets.

All of that said, I promise you, as you're suffering in front of those that love and care for you, or in front of new friends, new communities, or anyone with a heart, people are going to tell you what is good for you—but more often than not "you" is actually "them." And, as my mom once said, "you want to kick everyone." Don't be afraid to say no to their suggestions. You don't have to please anyone by taking their suggestion.

You need to be here for yourself, now, more than ever. The more you tend to yourself, the better you will be at being there for the people later, when they need you, too.

Over the course of the next six weeks my father started to forget things. Small things at first, and then bigger things. Important names, important dates, where he was, how to write an email, use a pen, and with time, how to walk. That didn't stop him, however, from using a phone, calling random work colleagues and speaking nonsensically, and getting into trouble. We had to confiscate his phone. It was becoming clear that my father was no longer in charge of himself. This was a shock. My father was fallible, losing his faculties, almost helpless. A new loss.

It took three hospitals to label the cause of his sudden brain decline.

I had lost my father as I knew him.

I found myself wanting someone to hold me. I wanted someone to listen to the pain. I wanted meals. I wanted help buying toilet paper. I wanted witness. Handholding. Someone I could love when the people I cared for most were slipping away. I called a friend who also was navigating parental illness to cry, to share this horrible news, and she started telling me what to do almost immediately. Even though I knew in my heart she only wanted to help, it left me more panicked, and less trusting of myself.

Was I doing everything wrong? Was I a bad daughter?

"You're going to have to move home now, Merissa," my friend spelled out. "You know that, right? And also, you better start going to yoga every single day or you won't be able to handle this. Every single day."

I wanted so badly for someone to have the remedy. To tell me what living my life should look like. To take me from the reality of Having-A-Father to Not-Having-A-Father with comfort, ease, and grace. So I listened.

My friend was a runner, every single day. I took her words as doctrine at first: "Yoga every damn day, Merissa." But when I couldn't get myself to a yoga class the words made it harder for me to sleep or cry because I blamed myself for having these bad feelings associated with grief, fearing death, missing people, being generally anxious all the time that I imagined a few warrior poses would fix.

Grief of this magnitude was bigger than not being able to go to exercise class. I found that hating myself for not doing downward dog every day made it harder to drop into the real sadness I was experiencing. Weeping was an important medicine in my grieving period, but I felt guilty for displaying my emotions and for not being a better daily exerciser. How had I accidentally let someone add a layer of guilt to my sadness? I didn't want to feel guilty for staying in bed when it was the very thing I needed most.

It did not take long for me to realize that my friend's system, her suggestion to do "yoga every damn day," was meant for *her* life. Her parameters. Her body. Her emotional capacity. Her spiritual work. Not mine.

It was a painful lesson to learn because it meant I couldn't turn friends into all-knowing parents. I couldn't behave like a child and have someone make all the decisions for me or tell me exactly what to do. I was going to have to listen, most deeply, to myself.

Your friends might need daily vigorous exercise, and you might not. Everyone is equipped differently, with different tools, different thresholds, and different support systems. She moved home; you might need to stay away. She had to go to work; you might need to quit your job. The parameters of loss, grief, and facing the horrors to come are individual.

What is important is to attempt to meet your own particular needs, and to do so in a realistic way.

I was also going to have to accept that while my friend got fit and thin running during her own hell of parental illness, I was going to slow down and thicken.

Fat was my medicine in grief. It gave me something to lean into. It was a visible marker of the change I was going through. It slowed me, paused me, brought me to where I actually was: sedentary, grieving, and needing extra thick cushioning and protection. To feed myself and be fed is to sustain my life, and there was at once this paradoxical element of jumping and pushing and banging my head against the fact that I needed food while my father's body was atrophying.

You may feel like you are trying to destroy yourself with all the things you are doing—all the ice cream you are eating and other habits you feel you are permanently picking up—but really, you're just grieving. Part of grieving means leaning on all the coping mechanisms, all the deepest most comfortable and comforting things from any era of our lives, and that's what's going on. You might have to regress to old comforts. Thirteen-year-old girl style. That young you was wise, too.

Stretching, walking, yoga—I didn't want a lot of these things because the more I did them the more my body woke up to the grief. They moved my feelings to the surface. I couldn't handle more than already moved through me each day. My friend needed to run every day to process her grief; I did not.

Try to find a way to lead yourself to water. If you can't handle the hardcore exercise, or the deepest meditation session, think about bringing yourself on a short daily walk or sitting in silence for a quick five minutes. Remembering your aliveness in doses will be helpful to riding the storms to come.

Recognize this path of grieving is going to be unpredictable, personal, complicated, gorgeous, and difficult. Accept, completely, the possibility of disorder. Grief does not have or follow any rules. It comes when it wants to, and leaves when you least expect. You are not in charge of what comes through you, what life hits you with, but you are in charge of you and your reactions.

To protect you, it is vital that you practice what I call "recognizing the rupture": Your business as usual is no longer. Your normal is altered. Disasters change the state of affairs. In the words of my wise friend Giulia, "Riding a bicycle might suddenly feel impossible." Go slow when slow feels right, speed up when that nurtures you. Listen to yourself. Always listen to your body.

I started doing simple daily check-ins, and I kept a laundry list of questions to get me through the days. You can make your own. Everyone's laundry list is different. Mine looked like this:

- Did you go outside today?
- Did you eat today?
- Did you drink water today?
- Did you move your body today?
- Did you pray/sing/meditate today?
- Did you connect with another human being today?

I started taking regular inventory of my basic needs and tried to do so before I was panicked, a privilege of circumstance, which required assessing what might set me off in advance. And I also started to take inventory of *who* was offering me care. I knew my love language. I knew what I wanted from a relationship with a partner. And because I didn't have one—someone meant to hold me, in sickness and in health—I was listing those desired qualities and taking the world by storm.

I wasn't going to wait for a prodigal life partner to rescue me from my grief, nor was I going to wait to grieve until this fairy tale began. I was going to work with the already abundant love surrounding me.

What's my love language? Presents. Easy. I was going to need a ton of presents.

And I was going to need all those things my imaginary husband was going to offer: hugs, care, toilet paper, meals, love, connection, all of it. So I wrote it down; I documented it. I chose to meet my needs instead of hating myself for not being married. For not having a perfect partner who I fantasized about absolving me of this crippling pain. I didn't have time to pity myself. I wouldn't keep beating myself up for not fitting into the socially prescribed role of wife and mother at thirty-seven.

I had a dying parent to navigate. A house to make a home. And a life to live.

IDENTIFYING YOUR NEEDS

Meeting our own most basic needs can elude us, on repeat. Forgotten needs left unmet can send us into tailspin. What is it that you need? A few ways to find out . . .

Five Needs, One Hand

- Think of five basics you need to check on regularly. When grieving, you will likely forget to do many of these things. Keep an eye on them. Identify them in advance. Check in on yourself. It won't stop the pain, but it can move it through faster, and/or mitigate how much it hijacks every arena of your life.

- Choose your five. For example, sleep, water, exercise, friends, protein.

- Stick with them. Assign them to your fingers, one for your pinky, one for your ring finger, middle finger, pointer finger, thumb. And, when the shit hits the fan, practice checking in with yourself. One, two, three, four, five. Are these basic needs met? Memorize them so your own hand is your steady reminder.

Wants vs. Needs

- Play around with finding what is really needed. Women are trained to suppress wants, needs, desires. In order to enter mourning, in order to grieve, in order to allow feelings to move through the body, we must at the very least be able to honor them.

- List wants, needs, all of it. Write down the wildest desire, the most basic need, the thing you feel ashamed for wanting. Maybe you feel you need foot rubs, or a pony, or an end to world hunger. Write it alllllllll down.

- Then rearrange the list. What is a want, and what is a need, or what is a want that, when sated, can help you meet your needs? What keeps you from falling apart? What holds you together? By meeting, knowing, recognizing, and labeling our needs, we can begin to get them met. When needs are met, you have more strength and space to feel.

- Meet some of your basic needs. Pamper yourself.

Primary Food vs. Secondary Food

- There are times (very few) in life where I forget to eat. When I do, it is because other needs, on deeper levels, are being met. Can you identify what feeds you?

Witness, listening, hugs, care, care packages? Cake, cookies, smoothies? What is the difference for you between food and nourishing actions?

- Make a list of foods you love to eat. Food is so important when grieving. Food is love. List the foods that delight you. I light up at the mention of Chocolate Therapy ice cream from Ben and Jerry's. Think about comfort foods, cooking as an act of tenderness, all of it. Just list what foods make you feel at home in your own body. Foods that root you. The foods that take you to some semblance of home, no matter where you wander. Food is medicine.

- And also list the things that you need to feed your spirit. Song, baths, parties, prayer, meditation, movies. List what feeds you, nurtures you. Keep these lists around. Keep yourself aware of the many ways you can meet your needs, or things you can ask for to meet them, at all times. When you forget yourself, come back to the list.

- Getting fed supports you in feeling your full array of feelings.

Time is hard to find for so many. These lists can be made on the bus, at your desk, while on the toilet, while on hold with whomever. Find a few minutes, steal them from your day. Make some lists. And check them twice.

CHAPTER 2

MAKING YOUR BED YOUR LOVER, AND OTHER TOOLS FOR NAVIGATING HELL

"WHY DID I KEEP STRESSING WHAT WAS AND WAS NOT NORMAL, WHEN NOTHING ABOUT IT WAS?"

—Joan Didion, *The Year of Magical Thinking*

My first trip home to see my father in the hospital was a disaster. My brother, heavy eyed, picked me up at the airport, and I could see in his affect how dire things were. After stopping for food and a change of clothes, and getting the 411 on my father's condition, David dropped me at the hospital and went home for a much-needed nap.

Hospitals make sickness real. Bed rest, loud beeping devices, bed pans, gowns, nervous fathers, overgrown beards, nonsensical sentences—I was facing this reality head on and I did not like what I was finding. I watched my father. He asked me things, like how the people on TV got in through the window, and was falling over and was on bed alarm and was balling fabric up in his hands nervously. My daddy was not aging exactly, but becoming childlike, and almost vacant.

This wasn't going away.

When I got home that night, exhausted, I climbed the stairs to my high school bedroom, which was much the same except the 1999 magazine-collaged walls were now painted over white. Same dresser. Same bed. Same books. Same photos of my friends and family. I brushed my teeth and put on my pajamas, eager, almost desperate, to sleep. And that night, my first night home after moving to New Orleans and seeing my father incapable of getting out of bed or forming a fully cohesive sentence, when I nested into bed and closed my eyes and drifted toward sleep, the bed literally snapped in half and broke. An Ikea bed, I believe, that was approximately twenty-three years old and had survived both my teenage years and the rowdiness of my twenties, chose this moment to decide to up and split. Right down the middle. In case I needed any more signs that my childhood was officially long over. Too tired to do anything, and too nervous to sleep anywhere but my cocoon of a room, I wedged myself onto the mattress, between the split sides, and I slept on the broken bed.

There wasn't much space for frills or complaints about bodies or beds or the newly developed crick in my neck from sleeping in a bed burrito. We got up quickly the next morning, picked up coffees, and committed to our major priority: being with my father and relieving my mother, who had spent the night with him at the hospital. We focused on trying to engage my father's mind, keeping him from being sad, bringing him back into this world.

I sat and watched him tap his foot to the rhythm of the musical finale of *Transparent*. I enjoyed the way he unfurled the newspaper, or arranged his snacks, or just the general look of total shock and excitement he got on his face when I entered the hospital room. No one else has ever looked at me with that strange raw mix of surprise and adoration. I held my father's hand, I sometimes stroked his cheeks, or just watched as he spoke litanies about Talmud or politics or the nature of the fruit he was eating.

When we were kids, if my mother asked, "Do you know where my wallet is?" my father would joke, "Look in the refrigerator." And if she said, "Do you know where my keys are?" The answer was, more often than not, "Ask George." And so throughout my childhood, George became this eccentric figure that none of us really understood. And as we got older, George actually became a character that lived inside of my father, that he would pull out when we least expected.

Sometimes, if my father and I were fighting (which honestly happened a lot, and I wasn't afraid, after his death, to admit that it was not all sunshine and roses 24/7), I would jokingly say, "George, what do you think of Allan's behavior?"—essentially summoning the power of my father's alter-ego. And George, always the peacemaker, would emerge: "Allan is being insensitive and incapable of really tuning into the intensity of emotion in this conversation."

I grew to love George, my ally, knowing this was just the deeper reflective part of my father. It amazed me, his ability to miraculously reflect at a moment's notice on the brazenness of his "other" self, Allan. George and Allan. My dads.

After two or three weeks in the hospital, and on a particularly low day, I asked, "Dad, where's George?" And he answered, "In my pocket." A few hours later, "Dad, where did George go?" He answered without looking up, "I never asked but I assume he's downstairs, in the basement."

George's absence was frightening to me. Another part of my father disappearing. I was losing every nuance of him. When I tried again, a few days later, "Dad, where is George?" My father was quiet for a long time, his eyes closed. Then he said, flat, "George is dead."

I was losing my dad in parts, piecemeal.

Every step of the way, every loss of an old element of my father, was more and more destabilizing.

We were courting my father's death.

In the hospital visitor's room, while my father napped my brother and I ordered an overnight delivery of a cheap metal bed frame. It was on the doorstep when we got home the next night. And when all we wanted to do was sleep—desperately—we dismantled my Ikea bed, the bed I had slept in for twenty-three years with my father down the hall, and tossed it to the curb. Then we sat on the carpet, my good brother and I, and diligently constructed my new and very ugly bed.

This bed was the future, a departure from youth, and just the beginning of the rest of this crazy experience. The pillows usually on my bed were, thanks to my own sticky fingers, now in New Orleans, so I got under the covers that night with an old tattered blanket and a pancake-flat pillow. I could almost feel the cold metal frame underneath me. My room felt empty, expired, like it hated me and wanted me to suffer.

When we talked as a family about care plans the following day, we agreed we would go in two-week cycles. As I attempted to cozy back into my high school bedroom that night, I thought, *Oh hell no I can't stay in this room. No. I can't live here.*

And then a little birdie voice whispered quietly in my ear, "Woman, you are going to have to."

When we are thrust into the most difficult scenarios of our lives, we must, with all our might, find everything and anything we can to make ourselves physically comfortable. We must make the bed a throne, rest sacred, and naps as frequent as possible. Bed must, in times of seemingly impossible distress, become an oasis. (When tight on funds, or time, this can be as simple as burning some incense or sage, spraying some perfume on your sheets, or simply changing out a pillowcase.)

I knew there wasn't a spouse in my room, like in my sister's and brother's high school bedrooms where they slept curled up with the person that loved them most. I knew this room, with this cold bed, was just not going to suffice in comforting me through this messy time. So I snuck out of the house and jetted to Bed, Bath and Beyond and made the best investment of my life. I bought massive oversized pillows, a new comforter, and strange things that brought me great comfort like an Ugg brand sock basket that felt deeply indulgent, and a lavender-scented eye pillow. I decided that if I was going to have to make this bed, and lie in it, and cry in it, I better feel comfortable.

When I returned to my parents' house, I entered through the garage, dodged my mother's somber dinner, and unwrapped everything quickly—making the bed, fluffing the pillows, tucking in edges and corners. Suddenly the crappy metal frame was invisible behind the fluff, and the new comforter was warmer, and, yes, comforting. It seemed to tell me, "You don't need to suffer any more than you already are; here, have a pseudo hotel room in your high school bedroom."

This gesture made me feel in control.

I reclaimed a space, made it mine, and turned its edges—shifting its meaning.

This was the do-anything-in-my-power-to-ease-this-pain grief, the tend-to-the-edges-before-the-full-storm-hits grief. I was preemptively making a bed for the woman in me whom I knew was en route—one shrouded in a grief so deep that she would not be able to function.

This act of reclaiming one's space is a power we can use in times of distress—prioritizing beauty, trading out old objects, turning the cushions, lighting the candles, dusting the mantle, relinquishing anything that brings detrimental feelings into a space that may otherwise feel nourishing. I felt like I had, most importantly, a loving haven where I could rest my pretty and exhausted head when hell, slowly, oozed throughout our home. Just the sight of my room remapped for comfort reminded me of my worth.

The objects we put in our rooms, by our doors, near our beds, in times of personal hell, they matter. Slippers. Blankets. Pillows. Sweaters. Anything to wrap us up, to allow us to feel held when the ice-cold blow of loss comes leaking in. Not only does this envelop us in tangible care, but it also mitigates conflict. Being comforted in any way possible allows us to turn down the angst and frustration and anger and fury that might accompany the pain of grief.

Bed became an altar to me, a place to worship the deserving, loved, divine elements of my grieving self. I didn't envy my siblings and their shared beds. I didn't want for much at all because I had taken care of comforting myself, honoring the notion that I deserved, even in the midst of all of this, to feel good.

Grief requires that you continue to be your own best friend. That you make your bed. That you pamper yourself in the ways you may have once held your breath hoping a partner would. And still, there will be days when without warning, we simply cannot get out of that bed. What do you do then?

Loss doesn't wait for good timing. It will come during a breakup or a divorce, when you break your foot, in the midst of ongoing oppressive forces. It won't wait for the right moment; it will sit with the other losses, drudge them up. Life, like death, is going to happen.

So, we begin with the basic: bed. Obviously we need more, much more, but these simple tangible actions are real, they are available to us at all times, and they make a difference, setting the stage for accessing deeper and more direct care later, when the time comes.

Bed is for rest. I learned this from my father. And resting in this bed you just made, when and if you can, is one ticket to navigating the trials and tribulations of grieving a great loss.

My father hardly stopped to say hello when he came home from work during the years it wasn't going well at his job. No kiss and hug—not until he went upstairs and prepared for dinner. Family time didn't begin, even though I heard the garage door, even though I saw him towering in the living room, his briefcase in hand, until after the nap. He sort of blew through the house, right upstairs, and took these amazing seven- to twelve-minute power naps that were imperative before dinner. My father took to his bed as respite daily. It got him through parenthood. He practiced rest in order to be a dad. (That practice, for the record, never ceased. He napped anywhere and every-where, and often when you least expected it.)

The way my father took to his bed was always the same. He was 6 feet 4 inches tall, his toes always peeked out from the bottom of the covers, his eyes were always covered by something—a towel, a pillowcase, an eye mask, and his arms were spread wide, like a king. He knew how to honor rest. How to use sleep as a tool. How to make his bed his throne.

My dad napped like royalty, and for all his shortcomings, this imperative he placed on his own rest was actually what probably saved all of us come dinner time. He allowed himself to metabolize his day, to rewire his circuits, to emerge a different per-son. We then, after the nap, got hugs.

Learning from the best of them, I made my bed a sanctuary during my father's decline. It was ready for me. Invest in your bed. Especially if you're single. Find new covers—they don't need to be expensive or fancy, just not awful. Get rid of those that remind you of the last relationship or trauma or bad job; start fresh with some new Costco sheets and a blanket that makes you feel like a divine being worthy of rest. Instead of waiting for someone to hold you, practice making your home a place you want to return to, that reminds you of your best self. Caring for yourself will give you a sense of self-worth, and having a sense of self-worth will help you meet, honor, tend to, and sate your needs and the needs of those you are supporting through loss. It will also put you in touch with your own need to ask for help.

Whether you buy from Craigslist, Goodwill, or Williams-Sonoma, it doesn't matter. It only matters that the objects and comforts in the room you rest in remind you of how loved you already are. Not just the bed, pillows, and blankets, but also what you see from the bed, what is on the walls, on the table beside you, resting on your dresser. What we look at influences us. If there's a picture of the high school boyfriend who broke your heart hanging on the wall by your bed, you aren't going to feel wonderful. If there's a reminder of your strength, you will. Clean out the room you grieve in. Make it come alive. Let it spark Marie Kondo joy deep within you so the descent into grief is less excruciating.

I had the following things arranged on a table by my bed, and they made all the difference: tinctures and teas mailed to me from an herbalist friend in California, soda water, three kinds of chocolate, and gifts like stones and shells from island friends seeking to comfort me. As silly or princess-like as those random things may seem, they were important emblems of thought and care from others. My friend Emily carried the water to me. My friend Julia custom made the tinctures. My friend Elysha prayed over the stones.

And when no one sent or bought me things, I gathered treasures on my own. I put meaningful, beautiful things in my sightline in order to honor and elevate myself, to feel as loved as my sister felt on the other side of the bedroom wall sleeping wrapped in the arms of her spouse.

These objects made my dated teenaged room at my parents' house look and feel like a spa. And it gave me a space of my own. An oasis and safe harbor. In the storm of family chaos—pushing my dad up and down the front driveway in a wheelchair, navigating relatives and their outbursts—having a sanctuary to return to mattered. No, it wasn't the broad arms of a man holding me in my bed; it was better: a space built specifically to remind me that I had sourced the care I needed, that my friends loved me and were on call, and that this small space was dedicated just to me and to my well-being. I was not lonely at night. I did not feel forgotten. I didn't even wish for someone else by my side. It felt good to stretch out. Like royalty.

In the aftermath of death, when I was tender, too tender for groups of people, my bed was the private space I allowed friends to visit. It was where they lay beside me, holding my hand when the pain was too much. It was where my cousin brought me breakfast in bed when I couldn't rise, where I ate a McDonald's hamburger when in desperate need of iron after fainting repeatedly. My sacred bed was where I cried, face to the wall, or slept for hours on end.

Bed was not just a place, but a practice.

It was a station to pause and to process, to metabolize this new landscape and reality, to digest and integrate the decline of a father. And something about the very act of lying down, and being swaddle-wrapped in blankets, was a signal, a marker, an exit from the mundane, and an entry into a space where permission was granted to pause, to process, to fall apart, to witness the reality of my grief.

This time in bed allows us, later, to get up and be good fathers, mothers, friends, people.

It is a time to be honored. Relished.

When I returned to New Orleans, I made my house a cocoon lit with love like I had done with my bed in my parents' house in DC. I picked flowers. I tended to the corners, got lamps from yard sales for the places where there was not enough light. I got plants, and kept them alive, and I made my home my nest. Or as my father so adamantly insisted when he scouted it with me, my sanctuary. It was a rigorous practice, turning the emptiness of a house into a place that held me emotionally, that reminded me of past homes and of my travels and of my deepest loved ones and most profound interests. And by extension, after making this space my own and filling it with my understanding of love, I found that welcoming my community and friends inside felt sacred, special, like I was ushering them into my heart.

Loving my home, being grateful for how it held me, and priming it for welcoming my emergent community made the missing romantic love feel inconsequential.

Some people don't have a room, let alone a home, of their own—a space to rearrange, a place to retreat to, or even the time or allowance to rest. This resting practice can be small. You can find a better pillow, a satin pillowcase, rose water to spray on your face when you lie down. You can travel with a beautiful cloth napkin and place it on any bedside table, or you can do something super basic, and simply clean under and around your bed to signify a shift. You can do whatever small thing indicates to you, visibly, that you care for yourself and you sanction your rest. Some sage on a shelf, a stone you adore, a note from a friend.

Try to honor your rest.

Even if you steal three minutes as a mom. Even if your naps are three minutes of breathing between hospital shifts. Even if rest is fleeting. It is yours. It is where you metabolize the hell that peppers life. It is vital.

Yes, learning to mourn and to grieve is a practice. We will experience another shock, another bad night, another sickness, another death, another handful of deaths. This is fact. Grief will return. And these practices won't take away the shock or the pain, but they lay grooves, small nests, paths toward a space of feeling, resting, and relieving our bodies of carrying so very much. I learned these tricks—the power of beauty and of rest—from my dad.

And . . . I had time to lie in bed. This is a luxury and rarely the case when any of us are grieving.

When someone grows ill, or any other kind of crisis or difficulty emerges in your life, it is good to familiarize yourself in advance with the allowances at your job for mental health days—the days, or short 15-minute stretches, you will take to your bed as a practice, if allowed. Maybe there are none—and if that's the case—all the more reason to build space into your free time for tending to your grief. And if you have no free time, perhaps fold these practices into private bathroom moments. Put flowers by the sink, a note of Louise Hay affirmation on the bathroom wall, so that while brushing your teeth or looking in the mirror, yes, even while you are on the toilet, you can experience love and presence as often as possible.

Your grief, in whatever way you choose, begs to be acknowledged.

Take time before the next spell of grief horror comes and assess a few things. Assess your own beliefs: What medicine do you believe in this year? Spiritual? Kaiser? Pfizer? I know it changes for me. Assess your wallet: Is there a budget of $10 or $10,000? What can you spend on your own well-being? 0$? $30? $300 a month? Without judging, or lamenting, get a fifty-cent notebook from CVS and assess yourself. Your finances. Your time commitments. Your health insurance or lack thereof. Your sick day allowances at work. Your kid's school schedule.

And then, assess your body. I do this in waves, checking all the needs. I have so many. I have bolts and grafted bone in my neck, screws and a cadaver's ligament in my left knee—I need a lot of extra care. We need to inquire: What is in my toolbox? What arsenal of healing modalities can I access when I start to feel like leaving my body, my world, my everything?

In New Orleans, while at first I quit my job for my family crisis, I later got another one. Like most people, in the midst of my many responsibilities in life, I had to make the time to grieve. I had to prioritize assessing needs, checking in with friends, building a support team, celebrating my wins, making my bed, sleeping in it whenever I could, and being sure to envelope my surroundings in beauty, in markers that I was cared for.

These are the practices that made grieving while single possible for me.

Grieving and making the space to do so was a great act of love.

SETTING UP YOUR GRIEF SUPPORT

Just like you might leave a list of care guidelines and emergency numbers for a babysitter, friend, or parent watching your child, make that list for you, so you remember how to care for yourself in an emergency. Things to do that are almost free:

- **List and notify trusted friends.** Identify trusting and available friends. Write their names down.

- **List and notify trusted family, chosen or otherwise.** Identify trusting and available family members. Write their names down.

- **Have an emergency contact.** In case you really panic. Pick one. Write the name and number down. Your contact can be a parent, friend, therapist, counselor, AA sponsor. Having this name on hand will make you feel so much less lonely in a crisis.

- **Honor your body.** When something is too much—as signaled by anxiety or nausea or pain or worry—walk away, stop reading, shut the screen, and respect your own boundaries so that you have reserves for what matters most. And forgive yourself for the times you can't. Jobs force many into ignoring feelings. And phone and screen obsession are typical in times of distress.

- **Get touched.** Have a lover? A nice friend? A roommate? Ask for a hug. Ask for a foot rub. Ask for them to brush your hair. Whatever. Just ask for some eye contact and some non-sexual care to ground you. There is nothing wrong with getting yourself a giant stuffed animal. No one to touch you? Consider a fifteen-minute chair massage at a salon. Let a stranger rub your neck or feet. It can help.

- **Bathe.** If you have a shower, get some $5 eucalyptus or lavender oil, toss it in there with the steam and bliss out—wash that pain out of your hair. Got a bath? Get Epsom salt, a candle. Just soak the rage right out of you.

- **Cry.** Yup. Hot forehead against the bathroom wall. Get. It. All. Out. Of. You.

- **Eat protein. Eat greens.** Not for your Paleo Keto fad diet, but for the sake of filling your body with nutrients. Doing so, may help calm you. Also consider rice and beans, anything grounding.

- **Drink tons of water.** Take your vitamin C, baby. Consider adding electrolytes. Replenish your adrenals. If it suits your system, get some magnesium. Talk to your doctor, and to your witch doctor, and figure out what's best for you right now. We can't make grief not hurt, but these efforts may make the pain move through you more easily.

- **Sleep.** When you can. As much as you can. Let your body metabolize what is happening. And respect your exhaustion when insomnia strikes—be patient, knowing lack of sleep will rattle your nerves.

- **Watch your own negative self-talk.** The "you suck for being so tired," or "you are a jerk for eating so much pie" comments. Tired is reasonable when grieving. Pie is comforting. Pet your own forehead. Go back to bed. Be nice. To you. Negative talk can also be a signal that you are more traumatized than you realize. Let it be a signal for the call for care. Whatever that care looks like for you.

- I really believe in the early stages of grief it is vital to **identify a "grief navigator,"** someone who knows more than you do about death and loss.

  - This can be a priest or a rabbi or a chaplain or a monk.

  - This can be a pro bono hospice grief counselor.

  - This can be a free community-led grief group, or a hospital grief group.

  - This can be leaning into the resources and support of the Modern Loss online community and other online collectives and support groups.

  - This can be a twelve-step program sponsor with the right tools.

  - This can be an emotionally available friend or family member who has already lived through what you are going through.

- **Swim.** Float. Be in some fake womb. Often. Public pool. Private pool. Gym pool. Bathtub. Neighbor's bathtub. Ocean. Pond. Find. Some. Water.

- **Don't pretend it's fine when it gets to a place where it isn't.** For some of you, pretending it is fine is a survival tactic that can't be forfeited. Don't judge that. I am not judging that. But be sure, when this occurs, be conscious of it and inch towards finding support in whatever way is available to you. Grandma, friend, coworker, therapist, hair stylist—whomever. Grief is horrifying. You are most likely going to need a leg up.

Things that (may) cost money (check with your insurance company in advance if you have it, or your Medicare/Medicaid—alternately, crowdfunding for your grief support is 100 percent allowed):

- A grief counselor, a therapist, **a professional to talk to**. You may need emotional maps. Better now than later, when it all catches up with you. Don't pile your pain. Face it with as many tools as you can muster.

- **A psychiatrist**. Medicine comes in many forms. A psychiatrist is the liason to not only complex understanding of the psyche, but also to the prescription drugs that may be the very things you need. To each their own. Any path to healing and caring for this rupture that is grief is wonderful.

- **Acupuncture** can help with nervous system stasis, and community clinics can cost as little as $10 a visit. Ask for ear and hand points. Some practitioners do trauma clinics with these points for free. Keep an eye out!

- **Craniosacral therapy** is sometimes available through hospitals with health insurance—this nervous system hands on technique was one of the best for me. It works for some, and not others. I found it calming and restorative as it lulled my nerves to rest. Consult your care team, your prayers, whomever you answer to before leaping in for this one.

- **Bodywork or Reflexology**. You can find this at a foot massage place or a nail salon for as little as ten minutes for $10, or from a bodyworker for as long as one to two hours. Price range: $10–$150. A little touch can go a long way for many when panicking.

- **Eye Movement Desensitization and Reprocessing (EMDR)**. This is a trauma re-regulation therapy for after a horror when nervous symptoms, flashbacks, outbursts, and beyond all feel out of control. A therapist usually administers this.

- **Somatic Experiencing**. This is extremely effective. Perhaps, in my opinion, the most effective post-trauma, post-loss therapy. It involves connecting the body and the emotions.

- **Dance/Art/Yoga Therapy**. Creative care.

- **Whatever you do, if you can afford to, do it for six months**. This time allows patterns to form, shifts to actually take place. It is long enough for you to move through your interior walls and to know if these methods are working. Consistency can teach us new grooves, new methods, new everything. And then, we grow.

CHAPTER 3

CO-PILOTS: MAKING YOUR FRIENDS YOUR SPOUSE

"BE MEASURED & FORTIFIED
LAUGH AT NOTHING DISCERNIBLE . . ."

—Akilah Oliver, *A Toast in the House of Friends* ("Wishes")

"The doctor called," my brother David told me in October, just two months after I arrived in New Orleans. "Dad has seven months. Ten, maybe." My father had just finished two weeks in a brain rehab unit specializing in brain swells. Rehab did nothing to improve his condition; in fact, he was atrophying. After weeks of tests, it was this lack of improvement with treatment that helped the doctors finally put two and two together.

"It's not encephalitis. It's a brain disease called Creutzfeldt-Jakob. One in a million get it."

My dad was terminally ill with a degenerative and rare brain disease often confused with a strand of mad cow disease referred to by the same name.

My father was going to die.

The night I learned he was fatally ill, I was invited through friends of friends to the Irish Channel for a weekly red beans and rice dinner gathering. I knew no one. In an unfamiliar living room plastered with photos of local parades and filled with people— performers, academics, waitresses, and writers—I was a mess. I couldn't put my phone down, a *faux pas* at a community dinner. I was getting texts from home and was in a steady panic. This was a new phase of grief all its own.

The host softly called me into the kitchen. I watched him take cornbread out of the oven on a skillet, then pour butter and honey over the top. He somehow pried my phone away from me as I confessed that I was having a rough time. I told him that my father was sick. That he was dying. Being alone with someone, being able to admit what was really happening, calmed my nerves.

I had never met this person before this evening.

How fragmented is too fragmented? How much are we allowed to crumble and fall apart and grieve before we're disinvited to dinner? How can we make friends when we are a total splintered mess? When to stay home, when to go out? When is it okay to tell a stranger the truth? And how much of the truth? I wish there were one blanket answer. For me, the ability to open up and tell the truth came, and comes, when a person is ready to hear it. My body says when it's okay to open up, and is clear about when it is not, by signaling me with physical discomfort or deep, sudden ease. Social rules? I can't tell you what those are for you where you stand, nor do I have a reputation for following them, but the rule here is to trust yourself and to do what feels good.

Always, when possible, try to do what feels good, unless at someone's expense.

The next weekend I found myself on iconic St. Charles Avenue at my first formal Second Line.

Classic New Orleans, the Second Line originated as a funerary ritual of the African American community that has been since adopted by the city at large over the years. Beginning with a jazz funeral, a band plays a slow dirge leading to a burial, setting a tone of deep mourning and sadness. The Second Line follows.

Derived from a combination of West African, Haitian, Creole, and American influences, a Second Line becomes a transition from sadness to joy, from absence to the celebration of a life and its ascent. After giving into grief and deep mourning, the slow hymns and the dirges, the funeral and the burial, the band ups the tempo and launches into boisterous celebration. What was once a funeral becomes a celebratory parade where attendees display dance moves in the Second Line, trailing the band. People ingather from all directions, many dressed in colors coded to their community, some riding low-slung motor bikes.

A guest witness to this powerful mourning practice, I walked past big trucks outfitted with makeshift bars, a man selling "War Punch" out of recycled milk bottles at a table nearby. This was New Orleans, another realm, where women in twenty-foot feather costumes, the queens, crowned, walked in the streets studded head to toe in beads and sequins and diamonds. Whatever part of my heart that was dormant, asleep, mute, was suddenly awakened. I felt I was enveloped by this practice, this display of opulence, the glory of the gaudy and the glamorous, an unabashed celebration of life.

I forgot the miserable news I was carrying.

I didn't know who had died, but I felt connected to them somehow. I was both forgetting and tapping into my personal grief, all at once. No longer alone, people bumped into me and smiled, welcomed me to the practice as I was folded into the crowd. There were the enormous tubas, gleaming trumpets, rattling snares—the Social and Leisure Clubs and white hats adorned with red ribbons—the dancers, oboes—all of it.

At the thumping glorious heart of the city, I suddenly wanted to share this experience with the person who helped make this incredible moment possible: my dad. So I Facetimed him, forgetting for just a moment that he was sick—that the end was coming. In the midst of the music, the crowds decked out in costumes, in the raucous fervor and the noise, I suddenly saw my father on the video.

"Dad!" I shouted, exuberant.

Usually if life was thrilling, my father leapt into the fray. But on the screen, he looked old. Disheveled. His usual excitement for any peek into a slice of life or exciting experience was overshadowed by how much the noise seemed to bother him. He quickly put his hand in front of the camera and hung up the call. It shocked me.

Where was my real dad? Who was this broken and fearful man?

The call shifted my mood dramatically. The people rubbing up against me in the street no longer felt fun or compelling. I was projecting my sadness onto the crowd. The magic spell of the Second Line was suddenly broken.

I veered off St. Charles Avenue, and I walked to a bench in front of a hospital and tried Facetiming him again, now in the quiet, in the calm, away from the noise.

My uncle answered this time, sheepish, trying to be a liaison between my father and me, which made me all the more alarmed. Why couldn't he speak for himself? Calmer now, my father just looked at me, ill, shell-shocked. He evoked a child being pushed in a wheelchair. I don't remember what was said between us. I simply remember the sob that lurched out of me the minute I hung up. Moved by the Second Line to see the truth, I suddenly let myself admit how very sick my father was and folded over in tears on the bench.

I had no map then. No guarantee that I would make friends, that I would find work, or community. I had no awareness that down the street was an old friend of my sister's who would become like family, or that I would be adopted by local chefs who would drop off meals. I was in the void, in the emptiness, in the pause before a storm, before the calm.

This meant I had to take action.

So I began with Facebook. I just looked up any friends, or friends of friends, in New Orleans, and I reached out. I connected with a woman I met at a retreat in Baltimore in 2017. I connected with two chefs my mother knew, and with a friend of a friend from DC who met me for Ramen at Kin and ended up linking me to her groups of friends when it was clear I needed company. I networked the shit out of New Orleans so I could build some semblance of a new community.

One Friday, I was invited to a Shabbat gathering in a massive old pink sanctuary where inside were tons of kind and welcoming people gathering for prayer and food. The actual pronounced theme of the night: "You belong here." My heart was filling.

Obviously, my style of introducing myself around a room to perfect strangers and taking their numbers to pursue them as friends isn't everyone's cup of tea, but the moral of the story is: When people make you feel good, reach out. When people feel energizing and kind, get their number. You really never know when you will need it.

Finding people you trust based on common intentions is a wonderful place to begin reaching out to form community, especially in times of change, new beginnings, and deep need. Examples might include gathering for hiking, gaming, sports, reality dating shows, or Shabbat gatherings, a church group, a meditation group, or a yoga community. New friends are exciting, they help loneliness wither away, and they help hold us steady as the hard blows of grief come our way.

I turned new acquaintances into fast friends: a woman named Julia, who also had experienced recent loss; a man named Gilad, who felt like family; and a rabbi named Josh, a friend of my most trusted friends who was deeply comforting in my grief. I asked them to hold the truth with me and they accepted. It was not a strategy, but a very important choice. I recognized empathy, availability, and strength, and leaned into my new friends by telling the whole truth about everything. They helped me get through the Zoom calls with my father. I was able to tell them about the lovely shock and joy on his face whenever I appeared, but also about the strange and cryptic wisdom he shared despite sometimes making little to no cognitive sense in our conversations ("If you want to fly like an eagle, you can't shit like a sparrow." True. True.).

This was a time of defining what I really wanted, and more importantly in this period, what I really needed, and I found these new friends were fulfilling all my wants and needs. I didn't want marriage. I didn't want prayers. I wanted cake. I wanted packages. I wanted people I loved to come over and lie with me on the all-weather porch and sweat and watch the tropical plants and lizards with me. I wanted visitors. I wanted macaroni and cheese. I wanted sex. I wanted movies and distractions and hand holding and so many bagels. I wanted more than a fake husband. I wanted people, my friends, to become a gathering place of all of this ideal partner's imagined qualities.

So, I wrote my own script and focused on the power of getting my unique needs met.

My one old friend in New Orleans, Kat, who would sit with me as I unpacked or cooked, was a steady presence and a bright light. My neighbors, whom I met just a few weeks prior, tended to me as their own, helped me take in the mail and water plants, and installed light fixtures and mirrors when I left town for long periods of time to be with my father. The simple neighborly waves from other porches fortified me, made the time alone at home feel less isolated. I wasn't by myself after all. The people I bought my house from wanted to take me to dinner. Savanah, another friend I knew before arriving and a New Orleans native, had urged me to let New Orleans in, to let the people love me. "It will surprise you," she said. She was right.

Years ago, I attended a writing residency in Provincetown, Massachusetts, in the dead of winter. When I arrived, I knew no one. Not a soul. But I'm a go big or go home kind of woman, and my birthday was coming up. I wasn't going to let celebrating my life fall by the wayside.

The local arts center hosted a party one freezing night, and I attended with a plan: I was going to make some friends. So, I walked from person to person, introduced myself, made a connection, shook hands earnestly. If I liked someone, even a little bit, I got their number. A week later it was my birthday. So, I took all of those numbers and conjured a party. I invited them all over for a macaroni and cheese extravaganza, and on February 10, around 7 p.m., ten people arrived and took off their sopping wet outer layers from the storm they had just walked through to help me celebrate, and nestled into my living room.

We ate Velveeta shells and cheese and Annie's white cheddar macaroni and cheese and Kraft macaroni and cheese in a battle of boxed pasta. At the time, I had an advice column called *Ask Your Yenta*, and we all sat around coming up with questions about sex and dating for the column. I got what I wanted: a birthday party. These strangers became my friends, opened up to me, sang happy birthday to me, and ushered me into a new year. This was my crowning achievement.

I decided to employ a similar strategy in New Orleans.

So, I went to work. I threw myself into community. I joined a religious group's planning committee, I started to go to a *Bachelorette* watching party, I joined a book club and a Mardi Gras krewe. Later, when things with my father worsened considerably, and my grief thickened, these groups, in the absence of intimate relationships, would be resting places when I desperately needed company. To the religious group I told the truth, I let them know my father was very sick, and they, as is the nature of such groups, offered care. And to the fun clubs, as I call them, I didn't mention my loss except on the rare occasion. I didn't mention my private family struggles, so those lighter fun spaces could be places of ease, pauses from the horror. I needed that kind of care as well. I was getting it.

A few things to remember, however: New friends can sometimes be complicated. You might think they are one type of person but could turn out to be another. They will disappoint in a way old friends don't, simply because you don't know them well yet. Old friends mess up all the time—we know them—so, it's easier to be realistic about expectations. My advice is to simply check your expectations and lead with clear, concrete intentions.

Is this a friend for movies? For meditation? For spiritual community? For drinking? For all of the above? Lay out your wants and needs before presenting them to the new people in your life. It will make navigating beginnings, especially in hard times, much easier on all of you.

I began making lists of who was making themselves available to me: new friends, old friends, community members, religious associates, and on and on. I kept these lists in the notes section on my phone, and the list changed every couple of weeks.

Category 1: Reliable Friends. People who are helpful and available.

Category 2: Reliable but Busy. Unavailable.

The second category was to remind me not to call them too much, or to not be disappointed when I didn't hear back. As time went on, I formed a third list for people who were comforting me in real and impactful ways and were clearly signed up for the long haul—people who were unafraid of showing up for what I was going through in full effect.

All the list making took five minutes, but in moments of panic, having these lists on hand made a big difference. I often referenced them when overwhelmed by emotion. I was building a world where, even in my aloneness, I did not feel alone.

Keep in mind that friend finding is like fishing. You don't get everything that bites (and not everyone is nice). It's fine. You will learn the limits of your people and community. Cut those losses and move on. This is not failure—this is simply a part of forming new relationships. Don't be deterred when it gets rough. Especially be patient if you are grieving *and* navigating new friends. You will likely be prickly at times, volatile toward others. The right people for you will stick with you.

Taking risks will not be all hunky-dory. No way. But it will, I promise, in the most unexpected ways, reap very important rewards.

When my father's health took a turn, and when I had enough information to know he was in major decline—this is when I wrote an email to my oldest friends. These were the people I would need as anchors, the ones I was comfortable crying on the phone with, the ones who knew my dad, and the ones who knew me before this sea change. I loved my new friends, but the old friends were the ones who would ground me in the tides of my grief.

You have all the permission to reach out to your loved ones, the anchors in your life, and to share what is happening for you. It will not be a burden to those that love you. For those that care for you it will be a gift to know that you are in a troubled time and need their support.

For me, the decision to send this email was steeped in self-love and in a basic recognition of the fact that I was on a dangerous slope; in a completely new city with a serious life crisis, even with new people around, I needed their grounding support to help me through. My siblings and I were sending separate updates to family friends about my father's health. This email I sent was separate. This was not about my family, and what they (we) needed as a collective support team: this was about me. This was an email I had to send knowing there wasn't a partner looking out for me, cooking for me, or helping contact people to care for me. This was me being my own loving partner.

I had to move through the judgment and fear that came with decades of conditioning not to grieve, not to make a big deal, not to be a burden. I needed to ditch the family script that judged me for being so open, for asking for so much. This openness saved me, fortified me, and kept me afloat through these rough seas. I sounded out the call to my most beloved people to gather closer. And it worked.

I put a toe in, tested the water. And from my outreach, the people came. And I had a community bringing me meals and dinners and laughter when my heart was just beginning to tank. I remember feeling scared, even embarrassed, when asking for help, and I remember feeling so relieved after I did. So I brought the care of the outside world into my new space, and in doing so I built a cocoon of love for my most grief-ridden hours.

Most people really want to be part of community, and the fact of the matter is, people love meeting needs and being there for others. That includes you. People want to love you. But if people feel inadequate or like they have to tiptoe around your emotional landmines with no map to safe engagement, they may find it hard to stick by you. They will need that map. People want to love us. People want to care. People are scared of death and grief and loss. People are scared of pain. And people just want to help make things easier. Generally, though, they don't know how. More often than not, with grief, people misstep.

I suggest offering tiers of care, multiple ways people can support you, easier options to acknowledge those also bearing large burdens of their own.

Offer boundaries.

Share what is happening with you emotionally.

Give them a map to your pleasure, to your needs, and to your heart. They will try and follow suit according to their capacity.

Here are a few possible ways to reach out.

> *Hi X,*
>
> *My dad is sick but not sure what's going on.* (List what feels right to share.)
> *Scary stuff. Just reaching out because I might need a bit more support than usual.*
> *This is harder than I anticipated.*
> *Thanks for being there. I appreciate having you in my life.*

And when things worsen, here is a template that might be useful for you:

> *Dear Friends I Love,*
>
> *New Orleans is so special, and I feel so lucky to be here in this amazing home.* (Give a positive, life affirming update to begin. Let them know you are still alive in a visceral way. Give them a piece to connect with: *for example: I am forming community and feel so grateful for all the change and growth and richness of place I am experiencing.*)
>
> *And . . . my father is still in the hospital.* (Here you can provide the update on your crisis. It could be: *"I was mugged last week and am having bad PTSD symptoms and need support,"* or, *"my divorce is harder on me than I expected, and I could really use more support,"* or, *"I am going through chemo and it's just awful. I would love some cheer."*)
>
> This is what I wrote: *He is in rehab now, re-learning to walk with balance and to regain his full cognition after a random and inexplicable brain inflammation occurred last month. Our family world is being remapped completely. My mother is now a caretaker. My sister and brother are managing his finances*

and his medical decisions, and I am in charge of the emotional damage control, emailing the masses, and helping answer a massive amount of strange emails and requests regarding my father's health.

(Now, you ask.) *I want to say I am perfect and fine, but I am also drenched in grief and am still only a month into a completely new life in a completely new world. It is very hard to manage this without all of you. And luckily, I have you.*

I need your support. (This is vital: be direct. List concrete real ways your friends can help. Many have no clue what to do with or for you, but they want to be there. Give them options, let them in, allow them to help. It will build community. It will build relationships. It will keep you floating.) *Here's what that looks like for me: A text, like Caroline has been doing, letting me know you are thinking of me. A five-minute call while feeding your baby, like Meg has been offering, or a call on your run, like Sarah has been offering, or a call on your way home from work like Molly has been offering.*

(Toss your people a bone. Help them understand you.) *Just talking to the people I love is really helpful as I move through the grief that comes with losing a version of your parent. I don't need to talk about sickness if that's hard, I don't need to talk about hospitals, I just need to connect with people I really love.*

And that means you.

(This is your hard time. The friends eager to support you will read the whole email, all ten pages of it, if that's what it takes. Shorter, though, is generally better. This is where you set your boundaries. As cultural critic, author and hip-hop journalist Joan Morgan says in her "Making Room for Grief" interview: "Boundaries are beautiful things right now." Write them out. Tell your people who you are and where you draw your lines.)

Things to avoid: Please don't ask more questions if I ask you not to. Questions, interruptions when I am trying to share about my family or even just my day can be super disorienting. I have so many relatives and parent-people calling and demanding answers, demanding information, in a time where there is no information really to share. His brain is fucked up, and we just don't know why. Wish we did, we don't. And we don't know if he will walk or think normally again or if this is the new business as usual. We just don't.

So giving me space to talk about the weather or This Is Us, *or, for those, like Irene, who have the skills to navigate this shit storm in depth, to just offer space for me to speak, to process, to get through—this is an enormous gift. If I don't call back, which you know is not like me, it means I don't have the bandwidth.*

Also, the biggest medicine: sharing your accomplishments, your joys, your love, your good news. It is weirdly soothing to hear about happiness and thriving. Spill your pleasures, please.

(And remember: This is not a list of demands. This is a request for care. So be kind, be gracious, and give thanks.)

Your love and support and patience mean the world as I hold it together for family, and also adjust to a new lizard-filled Louisiana life. Thank you for caring for me and being there.

With love, Merissa

(Add your address at the end. People may want to write to you, mail you things, drop food by.)

The first email I sent out, I was surprised by how many people wrote me back, grateful for the clear instructions. It worked. I got what I asked for. I got what I needed. I suddenly got calls, no questions, texts, packages, photos of babies for my fridge. The packages especially made a difference, the coming home to tangible care, the evidence of thought and action, the way those objects filled and adorned my home.

All of this said, it's important to know when to ask, and when not to ask.

It's better to write emails like these in times of acute need. Severe traumas like death and illness and violence—these are times you can assume are okay for bigger asks. Emails with requests that are amorphous or impossible to meet will fall on their hearts with a dull thud. Ask carefully and intentionally, and with personal clarity, and you shall receive. People feel good if they can fulfill a clear need.

And . . . people are suffering. Everyone is. Some more than others. Remember if they mess up, it's likely not because they want to hurt you but because their pain might be mixing with yours, or because they simply haven't known a loss like the one you know, can't understand the needs you have. Don't, like usual, force yourself to bend to others right now. Try not to be mean. People hate to feel they are disappointments or failing to meet your needs. Explain in "I" statements. "Hey, I am so grateful for your questions, for all you want to ask to support me. What feels good to me right now is not talking about my decaying father. It makes it really hard. Can we talk about rainbows and donuts? Thanks!"

It's okay to call friends and tell them you just really need them to listen today. It's okay, when dealing with severe crisis, to override other people's needs for your own—

but there's an art to doing so. Not mowing them down, but stating, in advance, what it is you are asking for. If they can offer it, wonderful, if not, move on. Try not to be angry when people don't have the tools to meet you where you are. Some people will love you and just not be able to be there. So many are not equipped for their own grief, let alone yours.

If they can't come with you where you are going, then close the door and knock elsewhere. They may have their own enormous loss, giant hurdle, sick parent to tend to. Let them be. This is your time. Some can't come along because they are also going through it, some are reluctant to grow themselves, some simply don't have the skills. Don't stop and evaluate the situation. It's your needs, right now, or the highway. Hit the ground running when they can't step up. Don't dwell. It's not about you.

And sometimes it is hard to say:

"I need less advice from you—and more listening."

"I know your grandma died in 1997 and it was hard for you, but right now, if it's OK, I need us to focus on my dad dying."

"I am so grateful that you brought me a cold salad, but my whole life feels cold, I am going to need us to go get Popeye's together because I need hot food. Can we go to Popeye's?"

"I am sorry to cancel again, I just really need space to cry. It isn't you. Can we reschedule?"

In these harder days, days of sick parents, of mortal fears, it's really important to put your own needs first and allow those in your life to decide. They will either come with you or stay on the sidelines. Their pick. You are not supposed to shelve your own comfort. You will be uncomfortable 90 percent of the time while grieving and have the right to ask people to step up, and out, for you. If they can't, they can't. But don't sit around with those who want you to flush what's good for you. Not only is this a painful time for you, but this is also, in my opinion, a sacred time of growth, of change, of deep engagement with the stuff of life and magic, and you are not to make choices, if possible, that wall you out, that block you from connecting to yourself, your world, your experience, and your loved ones.

Even in grief, there is love. Even in grief, there is magic. You deserve both.

In the late fall, I found myself harvesting all of the kumquats and lemons in my yard. My kitchen looked like I was running a citrus factory. As a way of giving thanks, I shared the bounty with my neighbors and new friends. I brought kumquats to the

Bachelorette watching party, gave them to the chefs that looked after me. These trees yielded a means of expressing my gratitude, extended arms from deep in the New Orleans earth out into my community. These were the harvest of my new life.

When I flew home to DC for my next visit, I filled an empty suitcase with Meyer lemons and tiny orange kumquats from my yard. It was just shy of 50 pounds. Upon my arrival I filled my family's kitchen with the fruits of my new life's labor: New Orleans sweetness.

My mother, brother, and I methodically preserved the lemons in twenty jars with an entire package of kosher salt. Soon these would be gifts for neighbors, for caretakers, for old friends loving all of us through the hardest time of our lives. Thank the people that love you in the way that is appropriate for you. Some people write notes. Others send texts, emails, gifts. You can do it your way—do it though, for them, and for you. Expressing gratitude, like asking for help, builds community. And community is just what you need right now.

SPECIAL REQUESTS: HOW TO ASK FOR SUPPORT

Special requests work best when asked succinctly and based on true needs. I know how hard it can be to ask for what you need. And, I know this builds community. Some people will flake out so hard it will shock you. Brush them aside, and move towards those that want to show up. They will appear. Cling to the good. Lean into the love. It will, I promise, appear. It just might not look like what you expected.

List of possible asks:

- *Can you come to the hospital with me on Tuesday?*

- *I am grieving and it's making me really lonely, want to make spaghetti together, not talk about death, and watch* The Office?

- *Would you like to have a coffee? I am struggling with what's going on with my family and wonder if you might have time to speak about it with me?*

- *We are getting a call about a diagnosis tonight, would you maybe keep me company when it comes in?*

- *Want to take a walk and talk about* The Bachelorette*?*

- *We are honoring my dad, want to come over and be a part of the memorial?*

- *I need some space, my dad is sick, could we connect when things have calmed down with my family?*

Lists to keep handy. I had one handwritten on my desk and one in my phone to carry with me.

- Friends who are available.

- Friends who are not.

- Friends who comfort you.

- Who offered to be there, and in what way, for when you need it.

Example: Someone offered to bring dinner. Someone offered company. Someone offered to go to the movies. Write it down so you feel more comfortable asking for what you need later, even if these things aren't what you need right now. What you don't feel cool asking for today might be the very thing you crave tomorrow.

Exes . . . who you can trust. Who you can't.

- A special note on exes: Careful on the exes slope. These once intimate people may feel comforting. But be mindful: you are vulnerable and open and they aren't who they once were to you, albeit familiar. And, they care about you and will want to meet your needs. They loved you once, and maybe still do, after all. But make sure it's acute needs, and not things that a romantic partner would do. They very well may ghost when you bring them into that territory, especially if already recoupled. Make them your dearest friends, they will show up. But stop at the mundane, and don't lean hard when it's no longer necessary, unless you want to fall back in love with a taken person. Friendly exes. That's. It.

CHAPTER 4

WHEN TO TINDER, WHEN NOT TO: DATING WHILE GRIEVING

"A GHOST IS A DUPLICATE, A TALL AND HANDSOME MAN WHO CONTRACTS THEN DILATES SO SWIFTLY, YOU CAN'T REFUSE."
—Bhanu Kapil, *Schizophrene*

I met a guy on a dating app when my father fell ill. I thought my dad was going to live. So I was like, let's have some fun, get my mind off of things! It was great. I felt confident, comfortable in my skin, and delighted to be delighted. And that was the wholeness of my intention: a delightful night. Nothing more. I was free. It worked.

But when he wanted to see me again, and this time my father was diagnosed as terminally ill, I moreso wanted someone to stroke and pet my hair as I cried, face to the pillow, rather than anything remotely sexy. This, for me, was the time to refrain from embracing (an online stranger). I had no desire, not even slightly, for casual encounters. That freedom I felt, the trust: It was gone. My wide-open wings were folded inward for the foreseeable future.

And I was weak. I let him come over despite my deeply knowing I did not want to see him.

Unlike me that night, you can be strong. Trust me.

Call a friend, tell them what's up, maybe ask someone to come over, and if it's your style, invite them to sleep over. Get on a Zoom call, reach out for fortification. I get so weak for men's needs. It's almost as if I was programmed to meet them and to override my own for the sake of male satisfaction. Hah. Funny that.

No. You don't have to sate his needs and forfeit your own (whatever gender your dating buddy is, whatever level of dominance). No, the other person isn't going to disappear or pop or fly off or die if you don't kiss them when they want a kiss. And if they do ghost you—they were certainly not worth it.

Your needs come first.

Period.

Especially when in the throes of grief and reckoning with great loss.

As this guy came over, as I forked over my personal space, I warned him. I told him, "My dad's gonna die." I told him I was emotional.

And when he arrived, I hated having him there. I hated this odd date for what he wasn't. I hated this casual encounter, and I hated wanting more intimacy from someone I didn't actually care about. I hated this emblem of connection and care that was a false model. His company made me feel deeply lonely. Deeply isolated.

This was a bad time to Tinder.

I was angry at myself: That space of loss was sacred and I had breached the boundaries protecting my sorrow. I needed my space for grief to sink in. Instead, I was knotted and tied up with this strange bedfellow.

Dating while grieving is complex, especially if you are grieving the loss of a partner, spouse, or other physically or emotionally and romantically intimate loved one; it is something that can lead to major chaos. Or deep comfort. Or both. This is about you. About what you can stomach. About honoring your fragility, your grief, and your vulnerability. And also about honoring your strength. Your desires. Your real needs.

Yes, the first step in a romantic, sexual, or casual relationship will have to involve honoring, considering, and not shelving your real, live, legitimate needs. This is the refrain of the grief and relationships song.

There *is* a time to Tinder—sometimes it's a great escape, a great delight, a time of needed, almost medicinal, connection. Sometimes it even yields real, loving, and joyous relationships.

And, there is a time to refrain from Tindering.

The only one who can know what is best for you is you.

Perhaps the real key to successful Tindering (and all other dating apps under the sun) while grieving is to work to learn and honor your desires. Lead with them. Are you seeking friendship? Are you ashamed of being single? Are you wanting sex to not feel the pain? Are you looking for a boyfriend? A sweetie? A husband? A poly lover? A baby daddy? A mommy? A dominatrix? Intimacy can be emotional, contractual, physical, sexual, platonic, committed, non-committed, all iterations on the full spectrum.

It's all okay—desire is okay—but for the desirous griever: Parse out your grief.

Parse out your intentions.

And honor your desires. One by one. Vulnerability associated with grief and loss makes dating very different terrain.

Respect your longings. Know they are heightened in this time of great distress. And try, if possible, not to chastise yourself for the helpless feeling of wanting sex when it doesn't appear to be available to you. (For the record: Sex is always available, just a matter of standards and circumstance. You can snap your fingers on any public bus and probably find someone to have their way with you. But what you want, what you need, and what your grandmother taught you that haunts you, are all very different things.)

Remember: Grief thrusts you into a different caliber of loneliness, one that is existential, deep, complex, and often leaves you desperate for touch, care, distraction, anything but remembering the grave. This is what all self-care practices are mitigating—the distracting pull of wanting to stop the pain, wanting to fill the void, which otherwise blocks our rational view of the situation. The Pentecostal minister roofer from next door is lovely, but is a relationship with him the one you would choose at your happiest? Do you want to be his third wife and bring his seventh child into the world? (If it's love, okay, it's love.)

Lonely is when alone feels like a curse.

Alone is when being alone is a relished, delicious time with oneself.

Huge difference.

Some people go in search of God when lonely. Others go in search of sex. (Many go in search of both.) Whatever it is you want, or don't want, to do is up to you. But understanding what drives your wants, what sex is offering or doing for you, this gives you agency over yourself and your experiences, especially in profoundly vulnerable times. Sex can be the drug that soothes the pain. And sex can be the very thing that throws you into a tailspin, breaks your balance, ties you to some wonky stranger that you never meant to bring so close into your life. Dating is best done when we lead with joy, not when driven by a desperate void to fill. It is best this way because we often lose our power when dependent on a stranger fulfilling our needs.

Fulfill your needs—call friends, talk out your problems, pamper yourself, eat well, compliment yourself, ground, masturbate, meditate, stretch, do whatever it is that feeds and nourishes and calms you *before* you go on the date. We often bottle up all of our complex needs and show up to a date wanting to be chill, but we ooze this desperate "save me" vibe.

We don't need saving. Not via romance.

Tend to yourself so the conversation, attention, connection, kissing, hand holding, sex, walk on the beach—whatever a date looks like to you—is a bonus, not a Band-aid. Preserve your autonomy, not as a wall, but as a permeable and vital fortress protecting the royalty that you are. We have the power to map our desires, map our longings, come to terms with what it is we seek. Because, as they say: What it is you seek; it is seeking you. Be it obliteration or exultation.

Example: I was crying my eyes out in the snowed-in silence of the woods years ago, when I texted a man I had met two months earlier.

"Hey," I wrote, "I don't know if this is weird to say, but I am grieving my grandmother and don't want to be alone and wonder if you might come over and sit with me."

It worked.

He did.

But, I accidentally fell in love with him. Maybe because he showed up when I needed love most. Maybe because when I cried about my grandmother, his eyes grew red and wet.

Grieving together, mourning together, crying together, really with anyone, is going to yield intimacy. There are no credentials needed for intimate emotional connection— just a willingness to open a heart. This guy opened his, and I opened mine, and you know what that meant? For the year to come, I was tethered to this guy. I was wrapped in his life, his world, his emotions, his drama, his karma, his family history, his everything. And everything about loving him took me further and further from my own center of gravity.

I lost my sense of self.

Moral of the story: Look before you leap. And take care of yourself before you go on a date. Are you projecting onto these strangers with absolutely no qualifications the ability to be as amazing as the person you lost? They very likely are not worthy of you, your love, or your sacred grief.

A big lure of dating apps is that being single inherently means less touch for a lot of people. Touch is a basic human want, a human need, a normal desire, and no one is bad for wanting to be touched, longing to be touched, missing being touched. These already frustrating longings can be amplified in times of grief. And this amplification can leave us very wonky in our choices.

It is not a sign of your social failure that you can't find someone to safely snuggle you, or adore you into the wee hours of the night and through the thick and thin of loss. Getting touch is very important, and recognizing this want and basic need can be so painful when meeting it feels so profoundly elusive. Remember, there are other ways of establishing feelings of connection besides touch—other ways of bridging out of that lonely void.

Because touch and being listened to and close to another is so vital, especially after someone you love is cold in a grave and gone, you might be inclined to override your better judgment for the sake of relief from the loneliness, from the pain, from the absence. To prevent this from happening, we must flex our muscle of recording and meeting our needs and setting our intentions.

It is you, first and foremost, who gets to be your partner through your grief, and for the rest of your life. And you are probably an amazing and wonderful person who is lucky to have you, and you, 'til death do you part.

So, parse out your needs. Before you Tinder.

Preempt building your dating profile by sating as many of those needs as you can, tending to yourself as much as you can, *before* you log on. It will give you autonomy, sovereignty, and allow you to have more choice in every encounter. The last thing you want is to feel beholden to a skeezy stranger who doesn't appeal to you at all, just because you are lonely and grieving.

Protect your sacred self.

Honor your desires.

Respect your longings.

Get on Tinder when you want. But the key, while grieving, is getting on with intention, with self-knowledge.

Sometimes sitting with others is enough to preempt loneliness. Another body in the room. A visit to a salon for two hours might be the thing that calms the nervous system. A friend on the sofa. I like making schedules of what happened in my day at the end of the day, a witness of my own life, as if reporting to another. We are learning who we are and what we need. For the loners among us, or those like myself who equally thrive off solitude and social butterfly time, it's so important to build in human contact, human time, basic presence with others during weeks of loss. Loss will blow cold air through your bones, the fixation on dead people will as well, so let the alive ones near you be with you.

Options for human touch, or how to ask for it, when you feel you can't have any:

- Self-love.* Yes. Be your own lover. Now is a really nice time to invest in good skin products, a new sparkly lotion for your legs and belly, a face mask, a vibrator, a self-massager, bubble bath. Tending to your own skin and own parts will make the need (or sense of desperation) for others lessen. This gives you more power as you choose who to date.

  *A note on pleasure: The older I get, the more I really understand that orgasms are not only nice, but necessary. I know many of you have never and may never have one—that's great too. This is just to say: Finding your own form of sexual release and admitting and honoring that you are a sexual being—whatever that means to you—likely will only work in your favor.

  - Don't wait for a date to define your sexuality.

  - It exists in every minute, every glorious moment of every day. Tap into it. Engage with it. And for those who are able to orgasm, this release, on a fairly regular basis, can be a vital part of honoring your womanhood. And if you can't orgasm, pleasure of any kind is also vital to honoring your womanhood, whatever that means (pleasure *and* womanhood) to you.

- Hugs. Hand holding. Being near others. Sitting and watching a movie with a friend. Asking someone to sleep over, platonically. It's okay to ask people, "Can you just hold me for a few minutes? I am really shaken up." And when you can't get held? Can't have guests?

- It is not weird to outsource touch. Tinder for some works, but it has some strings attached, like emotional upheaval, STDs, and general feelings of chaos when getting close to strangers while extremely emotionally vulnerable. Another option is getting a massage, getting a foot rub, getting your hair done, paying a stranger to touch you. There's nothing wrong with this: Supercuts can give you an $18 haircut and hot towel treatment and, for that time, someone is tending to you. Be creative. You deserve touch, and getting a little before logging on and swiping right can prevent you from making choices you regret later.

Building touch and care into our lives, especially self-touch and self-care, takes the pressure off. Tinder dates will be less fraught if you go in with less of a "need" and more of a "curiosity." Your freedom in the encounter hinges on this. And when you know what you seek, it is always easier to source it.

So what the fuck to do when not getting fucked? You make like a bee. You give your new neighbor some baked goods. You take a bike ride, buy a discount crop top (really). You take pictures of your body and share with a trusting friend, and you throw yourself, with abandon, into everything you love. Literally everything. You make love to the whole damn world. I can't handle the sexual desires I have when they come in, blazing, unless I write, or clean, or bike, or create, design, make a world anew. Send packages to friends I love. Glitter some toy dinosaurs. You name it.

This, too, is the work: channeling sexual energy. Channeling a desire for connection into falling in love with your world, your thigh and its majesty, the house or room or apartment you live in. I beautify as a practice, make my home an altar to my life, cook opulent breakfasts for one, dress up for no reason, dance around to Nikka Costa to remember a compass.

When I take my body—and all that flows through it—and harness it, when I remember this is my body, my life, the thirst and desperate misery of being a lonesome single woman disappears. Possibility becomes an infatuation. Allowing the unknown to arrive, setting intentions, lighting fires: The single witch grabs her broomstick and she soars.

Grief will remind us of the way we came into the world, and how we leave it. It will remind us that death lurks. Grief will break our hearts, our trust, tell us everyone might suddenly die or get sick, or that somehow everyone will fall to pieces. And sitting on the best and most well-lit velvet throne with all the grapes and gorgeous people in the world fanning you at your beck and call, in the throes of grief, you will still likely find yourself lonely.

As we wait in the wings, we can curl up and die. We can lament our very nature. Or we can grieve. And dance. And grieve. And dance. And date online, or in person, or not at all, until the next person comes begging for love at our doorstep. And even then, when they are perfect, a shining god, we can decide: yes. Or no.

There's no rule that you have to couple up.

This is real life, not *Love Island*.

DATING STANDARDS: THE NEW FRONTIER

Dating just ain't what it used to be. For you. This might be because you are coming back from a long-term relationship, tragically ended, or because you have simply been reborn through your process of loss and grief and mourning. You are not meant to emerge from grieving as you began. Normal may be completely altered. And so may the things you seek. New needs. New person.

Step 1: Work on knowing your desire. Map it. Write it. Use those old-school life visioning techniques. Channel some Oprah, Marianne Williamson, Shakti Gawain, Sonia and Sabrina Choquette Tully, intention setting vibes. Write your absolutes. Your make it or break its. Draw some standards. And, be ready to break them if the moment calls for it.

- Do you now need more tenderness? Someone more emotionally competent? Or was that always the case? It's important before downloading all the apps at once to **set your intentions.**

- **Write out your wants and your needs, again.** This time assess your state: Are you still grieving a death? A divorce? A horrific round of chemo? Be honest with yourself about these things. Know what you are seeking—sex? Love? Marriage? I generally get excited by other people's wants and needs. I am not the only one. This is a dangerous slope. It means, often, bypassing my own well-being. Don't fall for that trap! Try to learn your wants and needs first. And then put them out there in the dating world.

- This also will be amazing for how it helps you NOT date people that are below your personal standards, whatever they may be. **Give yourself permission to date with discretion**. Invite a friend over. Ask for help with your dating profile. Make this fun. Ask for blind dates. Sit at a cafe until someone remarkable walks by and give them your number. When you are ready, roar or tiptoe; wherever it is you are, however it is you feel, honor that.

- **Write out the qualities that someone you feel safe with and trust will possess**. Is it sobriety? Or is that a non-issue? Do you need an artist? Someone else with loss? Someone who shares your faith? Revisit your standards and desires, maybe with a friend. Make a list; look it over; tuck it into your bedside table.

Step 2: List the pressures upon you. Are others wanting you to fall in love so you don't look so sad? Do you feel guilty because your children lost their parent? Are you nineteen and convinced that you only have worth when loved and coupled? Are you sixty-five and convinced love is only for nineteen-year-olds? Error. List these pressures and then look closer: Are they about your own wants and needs? Or are they strange and often false narratives you have been fed somewhere along the way? Dating while grieving, it must be about you. Selfishly. Beautifully. Wonderfully. It's the only way. Love you. First.

Step 3: Continue to care for yourself. In every way. Don't wait for another person to complete you. Jerry McGuire wasn't that cool. You want to feel complete first; and again, the person you date, or don't, is a cherry on top of the fabulous sundae that you already are.

- **Be up-front with yourself about potential partners and your own romantic ambitions.** And also tend to your insecurities, to the cruel voices that say you are too fat, too ugly, too broken, too hairy, too impish, too brilliant to be loved. Self-esteem issues can be manifestations of grief repressed. Catalog the rough thoughts. Consider bringing them to a health professional or spiritual advisor or friend. Toss them in the river. Fill these spaces of self-loathing with care, especially when they result from severe trauma. You can't control the amassing of hurts, but what you do with that hurt, that is the power, and choice, you possess.

CHAPTER 5

WILLS AND BILLS AND THRILLS, OH MY!

"WE DON'T TALK EASILY ABOUT MONEY—ESPECIALLY WITHIN A FAMILY OR WITH CLOSE FRIENDS. AND SO THE EXCUSES AND COVER-UPS DEVELOP, AS WELL AS THE SILENCES, SECRETS, OR OUTRIGHT FABRICATIONS."

—Margaret Randall,
The Price You Pay: The Hidden Cost of Women's Relationship to Money

On the next visit to DC, it was my job to go through my father's home office when it was clear we would be taking over his affairs. He wasn't able to manage money, or doctor appointments, or flights anymore. We needed to start tracking everything, all of the accounts—whether he subscribed to Hulu, Netflix, or both, where he worked out, which gym to cancel—all the things. And it became my obsessive task, arranging piles of journals, bills, magazines, receipts, letters, photos, piles of pieces of my father's waning life. In some ways I loved it, because it made me feel close to him. I was able to sit on the floor of my father's study, off-limits until now, getting to know his interior worlds.

My father loved fancy things. He loved beauty and jewelry and fanciful objects so much it was annoying at times. Growing up lower working class in the Bronx, his family had a tradition of taking the subway to the Upper East Side on Sundays, and walking through the opulence of the neighborhoods, staring in the shop windows at things they could never afford. And as an adult man, my father's office, then in a brownstone in Dupont Circle, was filled with all the opulent things his family of origin couldn't have. It was nothing like the home he and my mother kept, a sort of shabby-chic collection of both new and imperfect vintage things. No, the office was Allan's space, where he collected antique vases and gold candelabras, glass tables and rare photographs. It was a shrine to his high taste, a departure from origin.

Not long before he died, when it was time to close the Dupont Circle office, he moved all of those objects into our family home in DC. His collection filled the garage. It spilled into the TV room. And the living room. Our house was overflowing with his odd things: archery arms guards (my father never shot a bow and arrow in his life), pinky rings, strange decorative knives and swords.

My mother begged my brother and me to come home and help when the objects came filing into the house—she needed someone else to reason with my father, to convince him to let go of what was excessive. And when we did make it home, we found two sets of lamps, new rugs under old sofas, layers and layers of tchotchkes. The house looked like a store. The fancy objects without the out-of-home office to display them suddenly looked absurd. Every trip home leading up to my father's decline, my brother and I tried to make the house look like the one we grew up in again, but there were new things, like fancy crystal decanters, amber glass owl vases, and ten-foot pink-tinted mirrors.

Sickness and death relinquished so many boundaries and forced us into contact with my father's most intimate worlds. These things he was so possessive of in life were suddenly up for grabs.

As I sorted the office piles, my cousins flew in. Trepidatious, I asked them if they would help. I was dividing things into piles: rolls of film, photo printing paper, lawsuit files, personal journals, magazine clippings, articles, family history documents, toothpicks (so many toothpicks), books of poetry, and the occasional orange peel, forgotten. The categories of my father's many selves were now divided and neatly sorted—poet, lawyer, father, husband, photographer.

It took only twelve trips and two cousins to move an entire lifetime of personal and legal documents to the basement. These acts of love from relatives—as simple and vital as carrying files—felt enormous to me. I didn't yearn for a partner or a spouse during this particular part of the process—I was consistently reminded that I was loved. I had different types of support that showed up moment to moment in ever-surprising ways.

Allow yourself to stop, look, and listen during this process of wills, bills, and later, after-death paperwork. You might find you have far more allies than you realize. Fear can block us from seeing the most unexpected people showing up to help along the way.

As a family, we decided on an order of command to navigate my father's worldly possessions, bills, and accounts. Because of this decision (and with the help of a couple of lawyers), the process was oddly swift and effective. I stayed out of medical and financial matters, bought groceries, cleaned and arranged the home. I helped with skills I had in my wheelhouse and was careful not to expend energy where others were already taking care of things.

When we found out my father was sick, my sister was the one to mobilize hospice care and important medical choices. My mother tended to the details of daily life and the work of staying by my father's side for every step of his decline. My brother was the one with the passwords, access to my father's personal documents, bills, and other outstanding matters.

Welcome to the paperwork phase of grief: Our lives are on paper and someone, whether it is you or your cousin, is going to have to deal with the pile.

Truth be told, well before my father's death, we had actually dealt with most of the logistics.

We knew where he would be buried.

We knew which funeral home.

We knew which funeral officiant.

We had a support network lined up: the meal train person, the grief therapist, a babysitter for my sister's twins.

Most importantly, we knew my father's wishes—for his body, for the home, and for most of his belongings.

We had the privilege of time and that made things very different than a sudden accident or unpredictable loss. This is absolutely not the norm. That said, there will always be the handling of paperwork and the arrangement of the funeral or other ceremonial preparations. And most people don't know anything about the particulars of organizing them until they're forced to take the reins and do it.

It is worth noting that once your loved one has passed on, their privacy oddly ceases to exist. Journals become fair game, bills, files, electronic and otherwise, that were once off limits are suddenly very accessible. Brace yourself for this potential responsibility.

Some of you will find secrets, unearth things you never wanted to know. And more importantly, things the deceased maybe never wanted you to know. Some will be big secrets, some small. If you're lucky, you'll find none. Without any sort of permission granted you may find yourself encountering the inner world and sanctum of another person. People contain multitudes, and in death we will unearth the good, the bad, and the ugly.

You and your family, or support team, will make your own choices about how to handle what you may or may not discover. Whatever boundaries were drawn in life may wholly disappear in death—revealing debts or great wealth, revealing second families or secret illnesses or mistresses or benevolent philanthropic donations, habits of all kinds.

Prepare yourself, steady yourself, ready yourself for this process being bigger and more complex than you had ever imagined it would be. Maybe your life is easy and manageable and organized, and all loose ends are perfectly tied. Good for you! Have a martini. But for the rest of us, this can be hard stuff because human beings tend to be messy. Two-dimensional relationships become five and seven dimensions. The hidden, the cleaned up, the tucked away, are revealed to be untucked, messy.

Systems that were set up to preserve order, to spare feelings, to compartmentalize wounds will be dissolved, and the complexity will mix with your grief. Tend those secrets like precious wounds, don't pretend they weren't real. Tend to all you discover before, during, and after death, and allow yourself time to parse out the wicked mix of love and anger, of longing and fury.

It's a lot.

Don't pretend it's not.

And pick your confidantes.

Assess the new landscape.

Make space for processing every angle of this cacophony to the best of your capacity.

Years before my father died, my sister casually asked me on a phone call where we were going to bury our parents. I was eating yogurt and berries and nearly spit them up. Last thing I wanted, in the world, was to think of my parents' mortality. I was annoyed she even contemplated them dying, "I don't want to talk about this!" I blurted. "Besides, it's not a good time . . ."

My sister was incredulous. Her father-in-law had just passed away, and she had been through every inch, all nine yards of death and mourning rituals. "There is no good time for this, Merissa! It's going to come and we're going to need to be ready." I hung up the phone, turned on *Love Island* and continued to eat my berries.

I had no idea how right she would turn out to be.

Paperwork is one of the most befuddling elements of losing a person you love, and perhaps the worst part is that it trails for at least a good year to follow. Without fail, after death, belongings, bills, death certificates, financial leftovers, debt, the selling of homes, cars, property transfers, succession fees, everything is far more complicated than anyone wants it to be. Don't be afraid to ask loved ones in your life about how they would like things dealt with should anything happen.

Apparently, when my father was dying, my mother left the one copy of the will in her car that broke down on the side of the road between home and hospital. When they finally tracked down the original, there was a mix-up in the copy job: Her will and his will were overlapping and therefore indistinguishable. What was my mother's will and what was my father's could not be deciphered. It was a mess.

Expect a mess.

These are emotional moments—deciding who is in charge of the deliberation of last wishes, who is next of kin, who is in charge of the estate, of the house, who is written in (or out) of the will . . . if one even exists. Some folks will quickly show flares of greed, whereas others will prove to be angels: This is a reckoning that isn't for the faint of heart. And death will not discriminate.

You will eventually also need death certificates, so many. I hated the calls I had to make to cancel flights, to tell the operator my dad was dead, to then have to prove it. "Can I send you the obituary?" Nope. They needed a formal death certificate. Some will suggest acquiring fifteen copies. I say get twenty. Who knows what you will need to prove and when, so make it easy on yourself.

Another tip: get passwords before people go. My brother had to hack into so many of my father's accounts, emails, cell phone, computers, to unfurl the details he was left in charge of tying up.

According to my amazing brother, David, when you have the luxury of knowing death is en route, here are some other things you will want to figure out:

- The will.
- Passwords, a list of all accounts, emails, subscriptions, prescriptions, everything.
- Is a lawyer needed? Who is the lawyer? Who is gonna pay this person?
- End of life desires. Life support? No life support? Hospice?
- Hospice care, finding the right people for the physical.
- Hospice care, finding the right people for the spiritual.
- Burial plans.
- Who will officiate the funeral?
- Chaplain care, repentance, preparation for dying, etc.

And when death is not a sudden arrival, when you have the luxury of time, a few special things to consider for final days.

- Flowers. I bought a peace lily and placed it beside my father's bed, and one day just filled the house with flowers. They will fill the house with smells and sights that are seasonal and vibrant. I suggest they be tossed immediately upon wilting.
- Haircut. Or any other soothing, dignified treatment to signify that their looks, their body, their life is still being witnessed. My 103-year-old grandmother put on lipstick up to the day she died.

- Meal. My grandmother refused to eat at the nursing home the night before she died. We realized that, in doing so, her last meal was at Cafe Pearl, a coffee shop named after her. Feed people with love in their final days if you can. It will make your heart, and theirs, feel good. This will comfort you later. I promise.

When it comes to material things, some people need a lot of time. It can be hard to let go of clothes, personal items, to clear out closets. Others want it gone, immediately. There is no right way, except to honor the circumstances, and also the feelings, both inside of you and surrounding you.

This basic caution and communication can help immeasurably. For some, there are house wars, family rifts, endless struggles for property rights. There is no foolproof way to avoid the storm, except maybe by listening: having talks with the dying (and the living) before all is said and done. Nobody wants beloved things to slip through the cracks or become emotional projectiles.

We don't generally talk in advance about dying—hence my balking at my sister's suggestion—and we don't speak ahead of death about the financial debris. Your loved one's financial mess, your family conflicts, the unearthing of decades of rifts, envy, competition, or resentment rising to the surface like curdled cream—this is normal.

Death mess is normal.

Planning, though, will possibly be your saving grace. My sister was right. Even if everyone is healthy. Even if you think no one will ever die. Having some basics worked out will potentially smooth things out later. The will in place. A lawyer on hand. Desires for emergency health situations mapped out. A person you trust for spiritual matters, funeral officiating, etc.

Asking people you care about what they want when they die seems nuts, but it may be liberating, fear relinquishing, and, in some cases, needed.

When it's too much, which it will be, instead of hurling insults or coffee cups, instead of jumping to conclusions or going to financial war, try to come back to yourself. "Pull into your bones," this was a healer's advice to me years ago. Just pull in and rest in your own bones. This means come back to you, the part of you that is at your center, that part that doesn't shift when the emotions ebb and flow, or the deaths come and pass. Remember the eternal buddy you have in your own skeleton. Drama and mayhem are temporary, but your bones are there before, during, and after.

As you prepare yourself for the enormity of the loss associated with death, and all of the details therein, don't lose you. Remember every little thing that brings you back. Try not to join the orbit of the unhinged—try and cling to your own mooring as everything collides. Fortify yourself, cling to your bones, and these enormous pulls and pushes will be less likely to tip your small and beautiful boat.

BUILDING AN AFTER-DEATH CHECKLIST

This is something you can make in advance if you have the time and space. This can also be for other occasions of loss besides death, like divorce, job severance, moving, etc. Lists can give you a sense of autonomy. They can give you a sense of power and control and order. Make them as often as it soothes you—but having one big, thick list for the hard seasons where you, most likely, will dip out, forget, leave your body, and gloss over vital details, will help keep you afloat.

- **The most important first step: What is your grief plan for you?** Map out your support team. Your emergency contact for when it gets too much. The counselor or group or priest or guru. Have those lists ready and made first and foremost. Who is your confidant? Who is available to help? Take the help.

- **Death arrangements.** Funeral home, crematorium, graveyard, officiant, flowers, etc. These are specific to each individual and each individual tradition, so navigate according to your community needs.

- **Costs.** Yikes. All of this can be too expensive for most. List costs. Think of how this will be paid for. Go Fund Me? Rich Uncle Bill? Aunt Rita? Hospital payment plans? Try and map it out, including the financial allies you may need—familial, institutional, communal—before you are struck with debilitating sadness.

- **Who is and is not allowed around the family, you, the sick person, whoever you want to protect, in times of hyper-emotionality?** This one is so important and so often overlooked in favor of more concrete details.

- **Who is allowed in the house when death arrives?** Your basic needs for space and comfort around the acuteness of loss, and those sacred moments of processing and witnessing death itself need to be protected. Make a list—talk to your family, or the team you have. Be in communication beforehand, if such a luxury of time and planning exists.

- **I promise that parsing out emotional needs in advance—when possible—will make it so much easier.** Just like a condom can prevent pregnancy and needs to be discussed or put on before the act, so too can emotional boundaries prevent explosions that can sometimes leave a mark for a lifetime.

- **Who are you notifying and in what order?** Who is first tier, for the privacy of the mourner? And second tier?

- **Who is handling the obituary?** Do you want an obituary?

- **Who is providing food?** You may or may not have to worry about that one depending on your community and situation. Who is caring for who? If this is something you are helping another with, consider listing their needs in consultation with them, and figuring out how you can help get those needs met. Any needs. All needs.

- **Rituals.** Who is in charge? Who is making the ceremony, the eulogies, the blanket?

- **Food.** Food. Food. I already said that. I know. This can be on the list like 100 times. Mourners will forget to eat. Feed them. Feed you. Who is helping? Is anyone? Asks are excellent now. People will want to help assuage this suffering. Food is an actionable way to assist.

- **Death certificates, property transfer documents, etc.** Make a list of all things related to transfers of logistical matter—is there a house? A car? A buggy? Find the paperwork, maybe even before someone dies. Get these wills, and bills, on track.

- **Government everything.** Pension, social security, benefits for the bereaved of any kind.

- **Money.** Credit cards, bank accounts, airline miles, points of any kind, memberships. Think gym membership. Think Smart TV subscription. Think of any wealth or debt related to anything. Run through the list of all these things. Share with your after-death team if you have one. If you don't, consider making one. This is easier when not done completely alone.

- **Markers.** Headstone, mausoleum, at-sea release ritual—whatever is your entombment, burial, ashes-to-the-wind practice, the final steps.

- **Celebration of life.** Build in celebration, after the destruction. It will make all the difference. Relish in what you loved about this person; and if you didn't, if they wronged you—celebrate your life, your strength. The point is: Celebrate life. As the memo we have received has made very clear: It is fleeting.

- **Thank you notes.** I am not 100 percent sure I believe in the obligation of writing thank you notes to those who write us comforting notes and letters, but for many this is a vital after death practice, one that builds community. I know my mother handwrote every single person—penning hundreds of letters, I believe—thanking them for comforting her. Thanking people, showing gratitude, acknowledging receipt of messages is one way to keep afloat after the death of a loved one.

CHAPTER 6

WHAT TO EXPECT WHEN YOU'RE EXPECTING (GRIEF)

"LOOK AND FEEL LIKE YOU'VE TAKEN A BEATING?"

—Heidi Murkoff, *What to Expect When You're Expecting*

For the week of Thanksgiving, my family gathered in a circle of love around my father. We had moved him home from the hospital and all respectfully took turns spending time alone with him. My time with him was in the afternoon, post-nap. I would climb in next to him in the hospital bed, set up beautifully by the window in what was once his home office. After his naps, I would look at my dad's face—red, round, different. He looked young, childlike, born new in some ways. He was helpless, but also so present. I wanted to climb into his mind and see the peace he was creating for himself.

I would ask him serious questions. "Do you have any regrets?" or "Do you love Mom?" or "Do you need any forgiving? Or is there anyone you want to forgive?"

It was a spell he cast in those weeks of November. Forgiveness permeated the lives of everyone around us. Estranged friends were suddenly close at hand. Feuds from work were resolved for him. The hardened corners of our hearts were growing soft.

We dressed my father in a fur hat and two coats and a blanket when he could no longer walk, and we pushed him like a king around the neighborhood. When his beard grew thick and wild, we called a really nice man named Antonio, from my father's old regular barbershop. Antonio spread a tarp on our front walkway and gave my dying father a dignified straight-razor shave in the sunlight on our front porch.

It was one of the most beautiful things I have ever watched.

The doctor had told us that my father had seven to ten months. But on a Friday in November, just a month after his terminal diagnosis, he started to act more and more strange—punchy—and soon he started hyperventilating. This shallow breathing was the first sign of a shift, that something was amiss, that my father was preparing himself for something enormous. He wasn't the type to panic. I knew then, seeing the vacancy in his eyes and the full sweat he broke into, that his life had become fragile.

The next day, Saturday, we were all exhausted, messed up in the head. I wore my pajamas all day. We were all spooked. Something, we knew, was coming.

Come Sunday, the house shifted. My mother went on a walk with friends, my cousins went sightseeing, another cousin flew back to Canada, my sister and her family flew back to California. The house was quiet again. I said good morning to my father, and I told him I loved him. He told me he loved me. He seemed to be removed from this world. I joined my best friend, Noah, and my cousin Nina in the living room—what had become the "waiting room." My brother, David, and my dad's hospice nurse, Ken, were in with my father when I heard my brother call out for me.

When I walked into my father's office, I saw that he was clearly having trouble breathing. The oxygen under his nose was not helping. I gently told David he could leave the room. Something deep inside me signaled I needed to be alone with my father.

David and Ken stayed on the far side of the closed door, on call as I took my father's hand and sang *Ozi V'zimrat Yah*, the Hebrew version of Psalm 118:14, Exodus 15:2, meaning, roughly, "My strength balanced with the song of the Divine will be my salvation." This calmed me, and I could tell David and Ken were taking it in, but my dad was still in need of more. I began singing *Oseh Shalom Bimromav*, meaning, "May the one who creates peace on high bring peace to us all." Holding eye contact, and much to my surprise, my father joined me, singing the words along with me.

He was suddenly lucid. I knew he could see me. I smiled. He smiled back, but I could tell it was forced. Something in him was beyond smiling.

Looking directly into his eyes I said, "Dad, what happens to branches? And trees? And what happens with the leaves in the winter? They fall down, and what then happens? The trees grow again."

And he looked at me straight in the eye and said, "The leaves have fallen."

"Dad, you have THREE BIG BRANCHES, me, Daniela, and David, and we are not going anywhere."

I could see on his face that something had shifted. He was getting ready to die.

I asked my brother to take over—the strong feeling in my gut returned, signaling me to leave.

I left the room. It was time.

A few minutes later David yelled out. I returned to find my dad staring blankly in a chair. We lifted him onto the bed. His breath left his body. I closed his eyes, sang the *Shema*, one of the holiest Jewish prayers citing unity and oneness, and then stepped away.

"I'm going to faint," I said. "I am going to faint."

As soon as my brother said, "No, not here, not in here!" I promptly passed out on the floor.

Like a pro.

My glorious, boisterous Renaissance man of a father, all six feet four inches of him, all the brilliance, all the knowledge, all the exuberance, died on December 1, 2019, in his own home. His heart just stopped. It was time to go. He died from deciding it was time to go.

That day began the rest of my life—forever changed by the loss of the man who helped bring me into existence. My world was now divided into a simple timeline: life before the death of my father and life after his death. I underwent a transformation from that instant onward that would alter my orientation to this world.

The body of my father would soon be underground.

Any death, any horror, any trauma will rupture the fabric of our lives. The clinging to "I want things back to normal" is strange wishful thinking because normal, before, included my father alive. That pre-Dad's death "normal" would not return, never ever again, because forevermore the new normal was life without a father. This is the time to say goodbye to "normal" and to not wait for it to resume. Normal as you know it has ceased to exist, and it will take time for a new normal to be born, in which your newly altered reality is integrated into the everyday basics of your life.

I knew rituals from a year of rabbi school classes, like pouring water out of all vessels when someone dies, and taking the body to the lowest place, and opening all the windows. We closed his eyes and mouth; we covered my father in his *tallis*, a Jewish prayer shawl.

And then I took a shower. I asked a friend for food. I called people. I sat on the concrete floor of the garage and primal scream wailed. I lay quiet. And then I joined my family. We called my sister. We called the rabbi who had been visiting my father and would lead the funeral.

After my father died, a potpourri of random people poured into the house. Not to comfort the mourners, but this wave was all kinds of people here to deal with the death itself. First the paramedics came, and later hospice came to declare him dead, and even police came to be sure there was no foul play. Okay.

Two women came from the sisterhood at our synagogue to be our liaisons with all details and any needs. This was not something I knew to expect, and I found it beautiful, useful, and kind. They came in and helped walk us through announcements of his death, through the ceremony, the burial, what happens with the body, all of it. And later the morgue came. It was really a liaison, three or four men from the funeral home that housed the morgue, but it felt gruesome, final, like the morgue itself was arriving. They took my dad away from us in a bag, on a gurney, draped in black fur.

Jewish tradition can include a burial committee that watches over, prays over, and bathes the body of the dead before preparing them for burial. Traditionally, we bury our dead within seven days of a death. I know some Jewish lineages believe praying over the body is to protect the soul of the dead, others believe it's an old practice based on protecting the body from rodents—every rabbi and sect will tell a different story.

My brother, knowing my father's body was alone at the morgue, went to the sofa set up for Jewish people to sit with their dead before burial. He read Whitman and guarded my father and reported to me there was another man there, hired by the synagogue, to sit vigil with the Jewish dead.

That first evening, we were quiet and requested no one be allowed in the house without permission. My sister had her wife. My brother had his. Sometime in the middle of the night, I climbed into my mother's bed, where we made quiet space to process our pain.

My friend Emily became my partner through the weeks before and after my father's death. She was on the "OK to be in the house in acute moments" list, something as a family we had to agree upon, and she was a remarkable friend. One of my biggest fears for years was being single at the moment of parental loss. I imagined being alone with my pain and feeling devastated, iced by the world. But that was not the case. Not even slightly.

In addition to family care and support, phone calls and texts from friends near and far, Emily came by every evening and always asked what I needed, wanted, and then brought me anything and everything I asked for. She was present, helped me pack, or chatted with me as I cleaned my room, or just lay there beside me and listened. She was the perfect friend in my time of mourning, taking amazing care of herself, and never making her problems mine.

I expected to feel single and cursed throughout the death of my father. But I didn't feel that way—not at all. I felt blessed, loved, and tended to by friends and community in ways I did not know were possible. People, I learned, wanted to be there, to make this pain less, to be close to me despite the prickly way my emotions permeated every conversation. I really think, with all my outsourcing, I wanted for nothing. In the midst of deep hurt, I found myself blessed.

Still, the next week of my life brought a grief I had not yet known—a cutting, biting, disorienting, discombobulating, world-spinning grief.

I passed out again in the hallway after therapy. My brother found me on the floor.

"Again?"

It was too much feeling.

I passed out in the kitchen. I passed out at the airport en route to the burial.

I hyperventilated.

I had night terrors.

I was a wreck.

Grief and mourning aren't things that can be controlled—despite what alcohol, drugs, and sex whisper to all of us in the night. Grief and mourning have a timeline of their own, arrive when they want, and come with a whole torrent of hell. They come in, then leave, only to return.

Over tea, a visiting neighbor told me she didn't fall apart when multiple family members died in a row. She told me she kept going, kept on with her life as the deaths happened—she was needed—there was no time or space to fall apart. In survival mode, she filed her grief away. Then, she told me, three years later, she began regularly collapsing into tears. Three years later, her grief arrived.

"There's no timeline," she reminded me. "No rules. There are no limits to grief."

If grief will have its way, whether we like it or very likely not, can we make space for grieving as a practice? Can grieving be a practice?

We can only brace for the possibilities to come. I could say, "Oh, I was ready for the grief—I knew my father was going to die," when he passed away in December. About my friends with terminally ill parents, I could say, "Well, they had time to prepare; this was expected." And yet, my father died and I passed out on the floor. These new symptoms are uninvited guests. We can't prepare fully for events that are shrouded in the unknown. The sacred.

A wise friend once told me that watching her father die prepared her for her first childbirth experience. There are parallels in the unknowns, the lack of power, the splitting between realms, and the ways in which a body and spirit are overtaken by the intensity of the experience itself. Similar to the preparation for birth, the terrain is predictable and yet a world of its own and different for each person.

My father's was a clean death. He died at home, a privilege. I was with him. It was natural. We got to bury him, eulogize him, sit with strangers for mourning rituals. I had quit my job. It was the holiday season. I had nowhere to be. I had all the space in the world to fall apart, to have loud panic attacks for a week that sounded like a honking goose, to fragment to such a point that my bed became my island. And despite these luxuries, grief is still not linear. Some nights I woke up screaming. There were moments I thought I would throw up but would instead fall down sobbing. My dad was dead.

I was in shock from not just losing him, but from watching him die.

I had all kinds of nervous symptoms of trauma . . . a different shade of grief.

Grief, in its many iterations, and the intense feelings that go with such an experience, are worth parsing out. The physical, the emotional, the spiritual, the conceptual, the relational components of loss, death, and the confrontation with mortality hit you on all fronts.

My brother and I met quietly the week after my father died to note the difference between those crying about the loss of our father and our added experience of being there in the acuteness of death and dying—the gurney, the paramedics, the witnessing of a body without life force. There was grief, and then there was trauma, and there was also this profound metaphysical transition we were privileged to witness and had very few tools to comprehend. We needed to admit to ourselves the weight of these layered experiences in order to navigate the weeks to come. We were there, in the room, seeing the very thing we were taught to pretend did not truly exist.

Death, we saw, was real.

And in its simplicity, it was still incomprehensible. Dad, where did you go?

This is a great time to call in your grief support team.

Whatever it is that your loss may be—a death, a divorce, an act of sexual violence, a crime against you, a financial blow, a shock of any other measure—the first step to stabilize the trauma symptoms is to acknowledge that you've been hormonally hijacked by a fight or flight reaction: an animal response to a threat. Then, you need to focus in and begin to use your tools, your baths, your bed, the grief support systems you mapped out. Now is the time to call the guru, the therapist, the shaman, the Reiki healer to address the symptoms or the shock at seeing something you may not have the tools to understand, or to assist with the welling pangs of acute loss.

Your body, mind, and spirit are in mayhem.

Your goal in the first few weeks is to come back to earth.

To return breathing to normal.

To stabilize the hormonal storm of trauma.

To calm the spirit, calm the panic.

Death and loss and grief can be hard on the body. I had digestive issues, extreme fatigue, pain everywhere. When death and loss tear at the normal fabric of your life, expect to exhibit a peacock display of new feelings and experiences for days, weeks, months, and, for some, even years to come. Here are a few symptoms that are normal for people experiencing shock, trauma, and loss: the cocktail of turmoil:

- Disorientation
- Forgetfulness
- An inability to focus
- Lethargy
- Crying
- Deep sadness
- Numbness
- Aversion to group gatherings
- Anger at the world
- Anger at the dead
- Anger at the living
- Strong urge to punch things
- Terrible sleep
- Massive insomnia
- Sleeping fifteen hours
- Dreams that feel like torture
- Night terrors in general
- Food issues, lack of hunger, desire to eat the whole cake, etc.
- Weight loss
- Weight gain
- Hypochondria
- Desire to never leave the house, ever again
- A fixation on your own death
- A fixation on everyone else's mortality
- Flashbacks
- Abrupt and unexpected crying spells

- Confusion about what is real
- Memories that suck the life out of you
- Clinging to memories that deeply comfort you
- Severe desire to protect the dead's legacy/memory/spirit
- Object hoarding
- Severe desire to beat up the dead for dying
- Conflicting emotions
- A wrestling with the loss of someone you love, and anger at things leftover from when they were alive
- A sense of helplessness
- Loss of trust in people, God, time, space, America
- An urge to have sex all the time
- A complete lack of interest in sex
- Bouts of inappropriate laughter
- Absentminded grocery store visits
- Heightened interest in astrology
- Renewed thirst for drama
- Fury for late night adventure
- Loathing and avoiding bathing
- Higher incidence of eating breakfast all day

Grief is everything and nothing. It is mournful, rageful, tender, violent. It is unpredictable and wild; it is soft and easy. And it comes in waves, links its tendrils to other losses, other griefs, other things that never got processed. Grief is this ever-present part of our world that needs tending. It is the neglected child of our times: We must feel the pain, or it will take over. Grief will have its way, whether we like it or not.

But can we be in relationship with the wild? Can we stay in contact with our own sadness enough that it lets us know when a break is needed, when a walk alone in the woods is necessary, when retreating to a room for a half hour to cry is a better idea than fucking a stranger from the internet with the same name as your dead father? Yes. Indeed. We can. Grief is something to build relationship with. Neglect will only make it louder, more attention-thirsty, more obnoxious. Make yourself a really cozy, loving, physical place to rest your weary eyes.

All we can do is learn these symptoms, become aware of them, and build up practices that will allow for them to move through us, to release, to find their proper home, wherever that may be.

Grief will change us.

If we let it.

And it's not just in our body that grief lives, but in our relationships, in our work, in our emotional worlds.

The truth is, basically, any big feeling out of the ordinary during times of great loss is probably grief. Grief, especially in our culture, is rarely about one single loss, one single death. Because we generally repress our sadness as a cultural practice, a little sadness can be a floodgate opening to the entire torrent of losses and deaths and unfelt misery and other emotions from many, many moons ago. Go easy on yourself. For like a year. At least. And it's important to note: If you experience none of the above, that's also totally fine.

There's no exact prescription for grief.

It can be awful. It can be fine. It happens now, or later—the only thing for certain is that it will happen, and then it will happen again. Whether this year or in ten. It might be that when your cat dies, you can finally cry about your grandmother's death—sure. But here, in these lists, are possible explanations for the very thing you may be inclined to pathologize, so keep your eyes open.

It's normal to feel like shit. It's also normal to find weird pockets of joy and meaning and excitement and connection in the void. It's normal to experience this broad spectrum of feelings.

Death may change you.

It changed me. I have new thresholds. New understandings.

Even new ties to my father.

Death. Is. Really. A. Very. Big. Deal.

And, at the same time, death is what it is: nothing at all.

Everyone dies.

The question remains: What to do with all of this, all of these conflicting feelings and emotions pulling at you? How will you cope with death in a culture that pretends we live forever?

We can begin by focusing on assuaging the panic attacks, nervous tics, and sporadic fainting—whatever your symptoms may be. Lean deep into food, and love, and rest, and community—whatever is available to you. This is the priority now.

Eventually, I scheduled a formal grief session with a hospice chaplain, and I vented and vented. I was filled with shame about things I did not understand—my stomach was doing flips; I was getting repeat vaginal infections; I was not able to sleep or focus or remember almost anything. I felt like an asshole for the way my life looked and felt it had collapsed into a mess. I felt it was all my fault. Instead of picking things apart, looking for patterns, therapizing these moments, offering nutritional advice or weight-loss plans or urging me to move my body, my grief counselor simply and gently reminded me I had seen death, experienced loss, and that these symptoms were normal.

This basic reminder shocked me because of how deeply obvious and deeply comforting it was. For whatever reason, I expected to be reprimanded. Instead, she told me a symptom of grief is obscure physical maladies because the feelings get stuck in the body. Oh! Suddenly, I was feeling empathy for myself. I expected her to try and teach me new ways. Or to tell me to get over it already. Instead, she was there to help me see and recognize the magnitude of what I had experienced.

My grief counselor made a huge difference for me. She just reminded me, over and over again, that my father was dead, and it was impacting everything. I don't think, without her help, I would have given myself permission to admit the breadth and depth of this loss.

My advice is to find someone who knows death and the experience of loss better than you do, let another remind you of the gravity of what you are going through. Those who haven't waded through the waters of mortality will not be able to navigate this terrain in the same way.

My advice is to find someone to talk about the underbelly of mortality with, and how to use this moment to your advantage, as a training ground for the rest of your life. Grief is a sacred turning point, and there is no going back. And that is okay.

UNDERSTANDING TRAUMA

Why do these clinical terms matter? They help explain a myriad of things we go through in witnessing death, in experiencing loss, in amassing symptoms over time. These terms don't need to be clinically DSM-slapped on to you to be useful. They are guideposts; they are signs; they explain the emotional and physical terrain of these fraught and horrifying times. And they explain why all the practices you have learned thus far work: They calm the parasympathetic nervous system; they settle you down from the panicked buzz you enacted to protect yourself from a threat that is no longer there. Or, for many, is. These terms may or may not apply to you, may or may not explain your symptoms, may or may not be tossed your way by a health professional. Death is easy for some, wretched for others, with a full spectrum in between. It helps, however, to know this language, to be equipped with this knowledge, to begin to have the tools to recognize when "too much" has arrived.

- **What is shock?** Shock shows up in all kinds of ways. Leaving your body, so to speak, staring blankly, or being unable to compute what is right in front of you. Shock will take you away from the present moment. Think of a kid who falls, gasps, stares about, and a few moments later, screams. The shock is that pause. It protects you when processing a horror that is just too much at that very moment.

- **What is it to "freeze"?** Like a deer caught in the headlights, freeze is an acute "stop, look, and listen" mechanism—animalistic—that allows a body to assess a threat. Do you feel shame for being helpless, inactive in a vital stressful moment? You may have in fact been assessing the very best and wisest option in that pause. Stillness can be a high state of being alert, or a simple catatonic moment of fear. It can also function as dissociation from a moment that is too intense for our nervous systems to calibrate.

- **What is "fight or flight"?** This is a built-in mechanism that helps the body assess whether to run or to rage when confronting a threatening entity. Think animals battling in the wild. "Fight or flight" commonly refers to the activities of your sympathetic nervous system, which toggles like a light switch with your parasympathetic nervous system (which controls "rest and digest" functions). This is an adaptation of the stress response to a mortal threat, and it triggers a flood of physiological reactions that equip you for battle or retreat. When it is triggered unnecessarily or will not subside, issues can arise in the nervous system.

- **What is fainting?** Fainting is a freeze symptom. Physically, it is a mechanism of the vasovagal syncope response, which can also induce vomiting and loss of bowel control. Think survival mechanisms. Think of your body as that of an animal. What is happening? The body is rejecting something horrific, toxic, repulsive—anything overwhelming or threatening that the system can't metabolize. Fainting is usually (though not always) harmless. It's good to keep track of your symptoms and share them with a health professional, just in case.

- **What is trauma?** Trauma is a buzzword these days and is tossed around with little attention to the actual meaning. It is a rupture in the fabric of the ordinary. We know, popularly, that it refers to something that shakes you up, leaves you scarred, upset. Simple. Not all stressful events will involve trauma, and the term is defined loosely among different healing practitioners. Not all deaths will be traumatizing. It depends on the situation, your emotional capacity at the time, the other factors in your life surrounding the event, your health, the conflicts around you, and so much more. For the very basics, according to the American Psychiatric Association, in addition to shock and denial, trauma can include, "unpredictable emotions, flashbacks, strained relationships and even physical symptoms like headaches or nausea."

- **What is PTSD?** PTSD, or post-traumatic stress disorder, was a term popularized after the Iraq war. You have likely seen shows talking about this idea in reference to after-war home life. It applies to a myriad of other shocking situations as well and is a condition that illustrates unresolved threats to the body and psyche—or fight or flight symptoms that can't subside. The American Psychiatric Association defines this as "an anxiety problem that develops in some people after extremely traumatic events, such as combat, crime, an accident or natural disaster. People with PTSD may relive the event via intrusive memories, flashbacks and nightmares; avoid anything that reminds them of the trauma; and have anxious feelings they didn't have before that are so intense their lives are disrupted." PTSD can arise from all kinds of stressors and events—death being one of them. It isn't necessarily going to show up—it isn't necessarily going to be a problem you have—but it is good to keep in mind after a grief-inducing experience. Also, calling it a problem negates its power. Fight or flight is a wise mechanism, your body's way of signaling alarm and working to protect itself.

- **What is Complex PTSD?** When the trauma, the threat, the rupture is not a singular event, but ongoing, complex PTSD can arise. Think microaggressions compounded with larger overt incidents of violence, or events that repeat and prevent the ability to heal, stabilize, or restore the nervous system. Fear can arise. Dissociation. An overall sense of removal from a shared reality.

Please don't perpetuate a culture of violence: if grief becomes too much for you, and only you can make this call, dial for help.

PART II

LIFE AFTER DEATH

**"I AM ACHING. I AM ALONE. IF ONLY I COULD
GIVE A BOURGEOIS PATINA OF MEANING TO THIS."**
—Dodie Bellamy, *The Letters of Mina Harker*

CHAPTER 7

WHEN THE FREE FLOW OF CAKE STOPS: RELATIONSHIPS AFTER LOSS

"IT IS A TERRIBLE THING TO SEE LOVE MISFIRE IN A MILLION DIFFERENT DIRECTIONS."

—Sarah M. Broom, *The Yellow House*

Witnessing death transformed me, and when I emerged, relationships were fresh and complicated terrain. I was new, as if in all ways I was beginning my life again. Same life, new vantage point. Could my old friends understand this emergent woman I was becoming, marked by such a profound loss?

My relationships were about to change.

From the moment we buried my father, Jewish communal mourning rites and time sanctions were put into place.

The pre-communal time of *aninut* begins when a close family member dies and ends when they are buried in the earth. *Aninut* is a time for shock to be remedied, for death in its acuteness to be processed, with a sole task of working to bury the dead and to prepare all funerary rites. This is a period when one is considered to be in a suspended state, outside of normal functional activities. It is not yet time for full rituals of communal comfort.

Cultures around the world each have their own funerary practices and mourning rituals, often bound to prescribed time periods, and these ceremonial rites are almost universally communal. During an NYU talk on Black grief, I learned from radio host and political commentator Esther Armah of One-Week Ceremonies in Ghana, Nine-

Nights celebrations in Caribbean cultures, and the black Southern tradition of memory jugs, to name just a few.

Burial is ideally performed, in Jewish tradition (and remember, Jewish practice and law varies between all the iterations of Judaism out there), within twenty-four hours to one week after death and marks the beginning of mourning in community. Generally, barring festival times and other possible exceptions, the first seven days after burial are called *shiva*, a time when the mourners are cared for and nourished by their communities, receding as much as possible from their normal daily life. They are meant to sit lower than others, to cancel all work functions as much as they are able, and, ideally, their most basic needs will be met by the community in this time.

The burial also marks the beginning of *aveilut*, a period of mourning that dictates how long one might practice saying the Mourner's *Kaddish*, a daily prayer for those in mourning. (Some believe this prayer is recited on behalf of the dead; others believe it is to raise the depleted spirits of those grieving; and still others might believe both, or neither, of these ideas. There are many iterations of Jewish practice and observance.) This period of being an *avel*, or mourner, lasts thirty days for the loss of a sibling, child, or spouse, and it continues for eleven months for the loss of a parent.

The first thirty days after burial are called *shloshim*. This period continues the staggered process of grieving—from *shiva*, the most intense phase, to the next, less intense (but still heightened) phase of mourning. During these thirty days, you return to functional daily life, but you are not yet a full member of joyful society. In strict Jewish sects, you don't go to parties, weddings, or listen to music while mourning. You are still permitted by ancient code to dwell in the depths of despair during this time.

Separated out from collective time cycles otherwise marked on the calendar, these prescribed phases offered me personalized checkpoints for my process of mourning. I was grateful to have them.

In the Jewish tradition that I was raised in—a strict but not Ultra-Orthodox iteration—mourners are told to remain at home for seven days after the burial of a close family member. People come to the mourners. They bring food. All kinds. My mother is a food writer; so in the days after we buried my father, chefs showed up with decadent challah bread pudding, Indian vegetarian food, Sephardic chicken soup, corned beef, Iraqi-style mujaddara, lox, bagels, Persian baklava, lasagna—everything.

I was a shut-in, and I was tended to, gathered around, cared for completely. *Kaddish* prayers were recited in our home in the evening. In fact, hundreds of people moved through our house over the course of a week, saying prayers, recalling great memories, and stuffing us with food. It was easy to make choices in those seven days, because they were made for me. No work. No travel. No nada. Supported exponentially, I sat with my grief, dropping deeply into it, a true privilege of time and space afforded me, during which I was able to remedy the symptoms I had of shock and trauma after seeing my dad die.

On the seventh day after his burial, ten people came to my parents' house to do a ceremonial walk that marks the transition from *shiva* to the rest of *shloshim*. It was our first outing as mourners. It was December and very cold. I remember everyone who was there: three of my mother's friends, my sister, my brother, my best friend and his mother, my sisters-in-law, and the rabbi who officiated the funeral. We did a walkabout in silence. Ten of us, dressed in black, around the DC neighborhood. It was solemn and, for me, scary: It was a coming out of sorts, a stepping out of this cocoon of care, a completion of the marked period of mourning.

I was panicked.

Do I go home?

Can I keep crying?

Can I fall apart?

Am I expected to resume my previous form?

What about my bed, can I still take to my bed?

Can I keep asking for help when I need it?

Is it weird that I feel completely confused?

What is this shame thing that has suddenly returned?

When is my sadness too much?

When, Freud, does mourning turn into melancholia?

Things moved so fast when *shiva* ended. My sister and her family flew home. My brother left soon after. A house filled with dozens and dozens of people was suddenly empty. Where there once were flowers and nurses and the enormous presence of my father at his soul's fulcrum, there was now emptiness. The house felt void, dead, inverted, awful, and no one really wanted to come over.

I tried to fly back to New Orleans, thinking I was ready, two weeks after my father died. I wasn't ready.

I found my proof in flashbacks that knocked the wind out of me and brought me, crying, to my knees. When I did the laundry and the machine stopped, the way it just ceased to spin provoked a vivid flashback of my father's breathing and heartbeat suddenly ceasing before my eyes. I slumped to the ground in my nook of a laundry room and just shook.

Want bananas in your cereal? No problem! But suddenly I'm in the kitchen remembering how my father used to leave his half-eaten bananas in the family fruit bowl, and then I'm cross-legged on the floor again, sobbing.

A few weeks after my father died, I returned again to DC to the comfort of family. When Christmas came, like good American Jews we went to the movies. And there, while getting popcorn, my brother pointed out that the man who was assigned to watch my dad's casket for days and nights before his burial was working at the ticket counter. I couldn't focus on the movie and pretended to go get some candy, but instead went in search of this man.

When I finally found him, I thanked him, deeply, for being with my dad and his spirit.

I was standing at a popcorn stand. At the movies. On Christmas.

My father's death was everywhere I went.

Even though burial rituals and visits to the mourners had ended, my grief was still very much alive.

Was it true that I was ready to stand alone?

Expect error, recalibration, to not know 100 percent what you need. Like a crying newborn, you are a wild landscape of new and unpredictable needs, and it's fair to not be able to foresee exactly how to soothe yourself in this early stage of everything-is-a-total-incomprehensible-emotionally-charged-messy-wild-horrible-touching-disaster grief. This lack of knowing your own internal terrain can wreak havoc on relationships.

There will be false starts. Forgive yourself—and then cocoon.

Climb into your bed. Pull the covers over your eyes. Get in the fetal position. Breathe.

When I stepped in error, I leaned, steady, into the timeline of grieving Judaism set up for me. You don't need to be Jewish to glean meaning from these time markers: like a semester in college, these periods of 7, 30, and 365 days helped me to calibrate my specific experience of mourning, to pause and re-evaluate shifts and changes within me, to mark the constant evolution. Having a slight handle on what I was going through, or a remedial map of the depth of mourning I was supposedly in, helped me find some peace in my relating to others—it helped me give myself permission to take space, ask for what I needed, and to rest where I could find pockets to do so.

I suggest marking time according to your markers of death, burial, cremation, birthday of the dead—whatever is your whim—and using those time markers to notice how your cycles of mourning shift. These time-based practices, older than me and my dad combined, bear wisdom. They are pivot points, markers of transition, and allow for places to pause, look around, and assess whether things have actually evolved. For me, at every marker, my grief certainly had evolved, until I felt *almost* normal again. This helped me process my grief in immeasurable ways.

Come January, one thirty-day grieving cycle after my father's burial, I resumed my life alone in New Orleans in my home. No one was sending packages anymore. The calls stopped. So did the food deliveries. Suddenly there's this territory with no funeral, no anniversary, and less coddling, less asking after you. I was on my own. I had to remember to eat. I had to remember to cook. I had to make my own tea.

I was on the phone with a friend while hunting my own desserts because cake stopped being delivered to me. No more carrot cake. No more babka. No more sweets on my doorstep at all.

"Maybe," he told me, "now that it's not showing up at your doorstep, it's time to stop eating the cake."

I hated him for saying it. I bought two cupcakes instead of one just to spite him.

But he was raising an important point: What do we do, how do we shift, when the immense amount of care for the griever subsides?

Cupcakes turned into a cautionary tale of the transition from excess to temperance, from the time to lie down, to the time to sit up.

I missed my family.

I missed being a griever that people cared for.

I felt suddenly very single and deeply alone.

I knew I needed to start calling on my strength again, and on the strength of my community.

Asking for help now, postmortem, post–life-altering loss of any kind, is different than it was earlier. People aren't going to sprint over with a casserole. They aren't crowd-funding for the funeral. They aren't even mobilizing for prayers. The acuteness of your needs have, at least to the naked eye, subsided—though that may very well not be true for you.

In fact, in my incubated state of extreme collapse, I had come up from the earth with a whole new part of me exposed and, as a result, had a whole new set of needs. Now, after the burial, after family time, alone in the netherworld of months two through nine after my father's death, when asking for support or needing it, I had to ask for new things, draw new curtains, and say no to things that used to be normal for me.

Be ready in the first few months after a great loss to greet your new self.

Be ready to embrace the shifts inside of you and the wildness to soon emerge.

Be ready for this to change your relationships, your needs, your asks, all of it.

Friendships after a death can be challenging.

The second month after his burial was a fraught time of no formal assistance and total fragmentation of my emotional world. Everything under the sun in my life had changed. My bed. My city. My job. My doctor. My friends. The immortality of my dad. And now the ebb and flow of baked goods and care packages too. The space of life after the death of a parent required recalibration at every single turn. Suddenly, I was in phase 567,884 of mourning. The last-week-was-hell-now-how-do-I-measure-this-less-intense-but-nonetheless-ridiculously-hard grieving stage.

And while I had just been taken to the brink, witnessed something life altering, and navigated the depths of my own despair, a lot of my friends had been going on with things at a normal, less intense pace. If we were the same before, now many of us were not. I lived alone, I did not want to also feel alone while speaking to my friends. I needed my experience of death honored, marked, and made space for inside of conversation.

Many friends who were by my side in my time of loss as my father was dying were less equipped to handle the landscape of after-death loss. Many of those who comforted me profoundly when my father was dying felt like foreigners once my father was actually dead. They didn't share my lived experience. And I felt they didn't have the tools to share equally in basic conversation: I knew the very thing I was going through was the biggest fear for so many. The loss of a parent is horrifying, and I was living it.

Thirsty for unfettered connection, and eager to dodge the possibility of handling other people's fear in the midst of a conversation about my life, I found myself asking close friends questions like, "Have you ever seen a dead person?" and "Have you ever been in the room when someone died?" I was separating out those who could understand the gravity of what I had been through, and those who could not. Those for whom projection or imagination was a means of connection, versus those who, deep in their gut, simply knew what I knew.

I called random people from my life, often not understanding why at first, only then to suddenly be deeply entwined in intimate conversations about the loss of a parent. It was as if I had a new sixth sense for those who knew what this pain was. And, a new aversion to those who did not.

Don't be ashamed of needing new company, or of finding that friends who were once comforting are suddenly out of touch with your reality.

You have gone through a sea change.

Rather than offering pithy (though kindly intended, I know) comfort, such as "your dad is still shining down on you," I wanted my company to just sit with the facts as I experienced them: My dad was dead. I didn't need to paint that with rose-colored glasses. I watched it happen. I buried him.

I remember when my friend Giulia's mother passed away, and I went over to her house with care items, hoping to comfort her. I also remember being terrified of her pain, so frightened by what I was seeing, and, consequently, terrible postmortem company. Not until my father died did I understand how medicinal fearlessness is for the griever, and how burdensome other people's terror becomes.

"All things happen for a reason."

"He can hear your prayers."

"Your father is in heaven now."

"Isn't it nice, he's up there with your grandparents!"

All said with good intentions, these ideas felt to me like side steps to the burden I was facing.

My dad's heart stopped beating in front of me.

My dad had made his last sound.

I closed his eyes.

I watched his body taken to a freezer.

I witnessed a massive concrete plate get lowered over his casket.

I scattered earth over his dead body.

I was concerned with the stuff of mortality. The basics of a Dead Dad. Anyone who wanted to convince me otherwise felt like they wanted to deny my reality.

"An odd byproduct of my loss is that I'm aware of being an embarrassment to everyone I meet," C. S. Lewis writes in *A Grief Observed*. "Perhaps the bereaved ought to be isolated in special settlements . . . To some I am worse than an embarrassment. I am death's head."

Grievers, like single people, are vectors.

They are vectors of the things we are taught to avoid, to loathe, to fear. In this case, it is parallel to the feared aloneness of the single woman. Grievers confront those they encounter with the prospect of:

- Death.
- Sadness.
- Suffering.

- Pain.
- Loneliness.
- Dead loved ones.

The funny part is: No one gets out alive, everyone will die, and yet we are asked to live in a fantasy where we do not admit death, nor the acute pain that follows for the living. Everyone on earth experiences this horror, yet we are not taught or trained to navigate the abyss.

The boundaries for what I could stand as well as what I wanted to guard had all changed . . . and that means the things that set me off had changed too. Like clockwork, conflict followed.

Volatile means "easily evaporated at normal temperatures." It means "liable to change rapidly and unpredictably, especially for the worse." As a volcano, and a very active one, myself, it was vital to try to mitigate the blending of my hurt with someone else's: Two people's trauma could so quickly become an unpredictable explosion. When my father died, I could only tolerate the most genuine, sweet, caring, loving people. If you were even slightly annoying, self-involved, dissociated, or anything but fully present to the sacredness of loss, I honestly excused myself from the room.

If someone rubbed me wrong, I went zero to one hundred in no time.

This is common after-death behavior.

Your loss, your trauma, and the death of a loved one, all will make you more easily moved to anger, frustration, and sadness. There is a roiling hell just under the surface that's likely always willing to bubble up and rattle your relationships. It's good to know that this chaos is coming, to plan for it, and to know that as scary as it may feel, and as strangely resistant as others may be at times, it is 100 percent OK to talk about it.

I had rage, and not just rage about the death and dying of my dad, but rage about old untended griefs galore. Old wounds, in this new bottom-of-the-barrel state of honesty, were raw and real and here and refusing to be hidden. Trauma will rattle the body. Death will shake the nerves and rip any veil, any secret loose.

What you could ignore before, good luck hiding now.

Plan for volatility.

And plan to prevent it.

Yes, even you can prevent emotional eruptions.

The more we treat grief and mourning like basic needs that must be met, the less, as my old landlords in Oakland cautioned me, "crazy gets to drive the bus." Would you put your furious three-year-old in the driver's seat and cruise through the city? Nope. You would keep them in the back seat and wait for the tantrum to subside. When we're grieving, we are at times like a tantruming child.

We need to do little *doable* things in this tender time to mitigate our proclivity towards explosion.

For example, I ate cake (duh) all the time when my dad was dying. I needed it. It was my drug. *And*, sugar makes me angrier than usual, quick to react. If I could go back in time, I would have added more vitamins to my regimen. I would have added more water. And maybe asked a friend to stretch with me a couple times a week. Something to break up the sugar's control over my emotions. But to not have sweets, in such a horrible time, that would have been too punishing.

Instead of unrealistically eschewing alcohol, sugar, or whatever your vice may be, (I support you and your twelve-step program too, this is not about sincere addiction, rather about temporary bad habits) buy a lot of water and keep it in the car for after hospital visits. Have protein bars, whatever vitamins and minerals are safe and fortifying for your system on hand. If you drink to cope, it will also increase the possibility of anger and reactivity. So balance whatever your vice is with remedies that lessen the possibility of volatile explosion. These little things could prevent a mountainous explosion, or at least reduce it to hill size.

Just because you are ready for a raw conversation, ripped open by death and loss, doesn't mean others in the room are, nor does it mean they have the emotional tools for said emotional conversing. Stay in your corner of the ring.

Go easy on others, and go easy on yourself. Save your sacred words, thoughts, reflections, and wisdom for those worthy of it, for those able to deeply hear your messages. And forgive yourself if you explode on occasion. You are hurting.

The best and most vital ingredient to relationships after a death are as follows:

1. Be realistic about your state of distress.
2. Be realistic about your wants and needs.
3. Be realistic about the actual emotional capacity of those you encounter.

Ask yourself, even in times of acute pain and deep loneliness: Why am I calling this friend? Do they have the tools within them to hear me, comfort me, meet me where I am?

Knowing in advance what it is that is driving you, and what it is you seek, will serve to protect you in your highly vulnerable state. Why are you calling them? Is it to fill the void of pain and sadness? Is it because they understand your experience? Is it because you know you can be with them in a quiet, real way? Or perhaps because you know they can be a positive distraction from the pain? Slow down before pushing send, before calling, and check in with yourself.

Come back to your five things. Sink into your bones.

You don't want to spend the days of sacred processing cleaning up emotional messes and navigating further guilt and shame on top of grief. You want to fall down, cocoon, release, and get the fuck back up again.

Hopefully, in time for next Mardi Gras.

SETTING NEW BOUNDARIES

- **What is a boundary?** According to educator, activist, and researcher McKensie Mack, "Boundary Work™ is the practice of acting on our right to decide when and how our physical, mental and emotional capacity will be used and for what purpose."

  - This is more than just saying no or refusing to do things that make us profoundly uncomfortable when already living in a state of discomfort, it is an act of protecting sacred inner space, of making choices and speaking limits out loud, of allowing room within us to go through the work of grief and mourning.

- **Why do boundaries matter more in times of grief?** We are vulnerable when we grieve. Tender in new ways. Parts of us we spent years shielding and protecting and refusing to touch might suddenly be raw and exposed. This is a time that warrants protecting, and also a time that likely demands so much strength and hard work in new ways. This hard work also deserves to be honored and protected and given ample space. Don't wait for someone else to protect you. You are the protector now.

- **Setting boundaries is really about stating needs** and being honest with ourselves about where we are, in this moment, and how that changes over time. This work is about learning to articulate your new realm of expectations now that you are profoundly vulnerable in unexpected ways. This is very hard for a lot of people. Some who can't set boundaries for themselves will resent you as you do the good work. This is not your problem.

- **How to say no.** Build boundaries, not walls. Learn how to say, "I can't be there for you," and know what to expect when someone hates you for it. Saying no and pulling inwards, as long as the risk is not too great, is encouraged. When asking for new things or making requests, it is good to lead with genuine positivity and praise. Try, "I appreciate you and all you do for me," or, "Hey, I love you and want to be there for you. And . . . to be honest, I don't have the capacity right now to support you in the way you need." Followed by the ask, "Right now, I am hanging on by a thread and want to wait until I have my reserves ready to be fully present with you. Can we wait to have this conversation?" And then, praise again. "Thank you for loving me and understanding."

- **People will often retaliate when you set limits to protect yourself.** Saying no to things we used to always say yes to will shock a lot of people, and it will make people who don't understand the depth of your experience angry. Know their rage is more often than not about their own weird issues and is not your problem. They probably feel rejected by you, and hopefully that praise sandwich will mitigate that factor. As long as you are honest in stating your need, not demanding, but cuing them into where you are at and why you need what you need, if they are the right friend for you now, they will understand.

- **Calibrate when the reactions of others don't meet the gravity of the moment, and step away.** Let them deal with their own internal stuff. Now is not the time for helping others grow. Now is the time to tend to you. This will benefit your relationships in the long run. The last thing we need is drama. Their anger is not your problem. Step away.

- **What are you protecting?** This includes personal expectations of self-care, drawing a salty circle around the practices that protect you, letting housemates know, "Hey, I need like fifteen minutes for meditation," honoring the vital need for a walk, or protecting your nap—all fifteen sacred minutes. The less you draw boundaries, the more likely you are to explode. At a Jewish wedding, the bride and groom circle one another seven times. Circle yourself. This work is about circling and protecting the sphere that is you.

- **Boundaries are about caring.** Not fighting. To remind you that you are worthy of these limits set to protect, guard, and grow the best parts of you, you could buy body oil and, as a practice in the morning, rub sacred oil into your sacred skin as you meditate for five minutes on the sacred limits you need in your life right now to protect the sacred process of your growth.

CHAPTER 8

HELLO?
IS THIS OVER YET?

**"TO DESIGNATE A HELL IS NOT, OF COURSE, TO TELL US ANYTHING
ABOUT HOW TO EXTRACT PEOPLE FROM THAT HELL,
HOW TO MODERATE HELL'S FLAMES."**

—Susan Sontag, *Regarding the Pain of Others*

Come February, just two months after my father died, I was gearing up for my first Mardi Gras. I had a new job. I had an old wedding dress my father bought me for $25 as a joke years earlier when a bridal shop went out of business. I spent my evenings after work painting it, deconstructing it, gluing flowers and stitching beads to make this my Mardi Gras costume.

Leading up to Fat Tuesday I wrestled with contradicting beliefs within myself. My religion told me to pause the party, to stop for this time of *aveilut*, of mourning, to avoid dancing, joy, and the like. One year—this time allowance belongs to the stricter realm of Jewish tradition—one year away from the regular joys of the world when a parent dies, and then you return. I remember my uncle telling me how some of his patients needed a year of sleep to recover from certain things. I remember a Jewish agricultural concept of the *shmita* year—after six years of growth, taking a seventh year to leave the field arid, to leave the field quiet, to let it find its way to regeneration.

The idea of a year off, of a year to pause, of a year for mourning in which I would participate wholly differently in life was hard for me to submit to.

On a Friday, I joined my krewe, Krewe of Dystopian Paradise, for a pre–Mardi Gras parade called La Boheme, wearing a velour onesie, sparkly leggings, a decked-out hot-pink blazer, and hiking boots. When we began to ride through crowds for two miles—essentially a slow boisterous walk, dance, bike ride, float moving through roaring throngs of people from the Bywater through the Marigny to the French Quarter—I was both happy and bewildered, both excited and exhausted. I felt like a minor celebrity dance star, and at once aware of the haunted unlit corners of New Orleans streets.

I said I was happy. My body was flailing in celebration. But inside, I had the sense that my knowledge of death was shadowing my walk through the city. I was half there—pushing into joy with all my might while another part of me wholly resisted. I felt guilty for parading, guilty for dancing, guilty for getting up and going when I was taught otherwise. I wasn't afraid of God, per se, but I was worried about consequences.

Perhaps, for me, as someone new to New Orleans, drinking and frolicking was more dangerous when one leg was so close to the grave.

I felt a pop in my left knee. I kept on keeping on. And then, as we got about two feet away from the French Quarter, I felt this burst of excited energy in my legs, leapt into the air, and I landed in some strange squat of a dance move, screamed and fell into the onlooking crowd. Lovely. I partially tore my ACL, and flipped my meniscus, causing a massive bucket tear.

Yeah. This was not my time to dance.

"To everything there is a season, and a time to every purpose," right? "A time to be born, and a time to die; a time to plant, and a time to pluck up that which is planted." OK. And of course, "A time to break down, and a time to build up; A time to weep, and a time to laugh; A time to mourn, and a time to dance."

I rode the St. Anne's Mardi Gras Day parade in my deconstructed wedding dress on a bike taxi, leg in an ankle-to-thigh brace, crutches hanging over the edge. And my body took me to a sofa for the months to come. Whether I liked it or not, this was going to have to be my time to mourn.

Moored at home, alone (except for the fifty-three days my mother joined me post knee surgery), I got sick of my resurging waves of grief. Distractions were few and far between, and a litany played in my head over and over to remind me that my father was dead. A sticky note to the forehead. Good morning, your dear daddy died months ago. Good afternoon, Merissa, you can't call your papa because he died. He looked so alive in photos. My brain was cloudy.

I kept thinking about how one winter in Johnson, Vermont, at the Studio Center, a student from the local college asked to intern with me. The young man told me he had recently lost his mother. One day, he showed up to the coffeeshop where we discussed work. His knuckles were bloody. Later that day, I spoke to my wise friend, Maria, and told her how shocked I was that he showed up with his raw flesh ripped up.

"Yeah," she said, matter of fact. "He was punching walls. His mom died. It's what people do."

I thought it was scary and strange then. And now that my father is dead, I get it.

Before I found a grief group, I had begun to isolate myself and draw the curtains. I was growing very dim.

I stopped telling people about waking up to a felt sense that my father was in my room. I didn't mention how at the City Park Sculpture Garden the pieces of art made me think of him, and it made me want to smash them. I didn't tell people about evenings spent watching a TV show about underwater wars between sharks and octopuses. How thinking of my father enjoying this made me realize he was dead, again, and again, and again. Angry to a point of near fury, I had to hold my own hand steady so I wouldn't toss my coffee mug through the glass window.

I wanted to smash things. To rage. To scream. To break fine art to pieces and bludgeon trees as if they had blood to pour out.

Anger, it seemed, had moved in.

I had the urge to drop wine glasses down staircases, to pop balloons, to punch walls. I highly recommend batting cages for getting this anger out of the body; but also, break plates, get yourself a piñata, bang on pots and pans, ring bells, yell out the car window to no one—anything to get this out.

Anger is movement. That which was dormant is now alive, that which was lying down is now raging, standing up and screaming.

I was furious at my body for breaking down. I was furious at my father for dying. I was furious at everything he did while he was alive that I didn't like. I was furious that I loved him. Furious that I missed him. I was angry at the moon, at the stars, at my pain. When it welled up in me, I wanted to break and smash and just obliterate the world around me.

Where the fuck was my dad?

And, as we all know, anger begets anger begets anger.

You know the scene at the end of *Carrie*? When everything is fine. Everything is copacetic. It isn't just *Carrie*. It's every horror movie. Where you are like, phew, that hellstorm is over. Phew. Everyone's safe.

And then BOOM! Jack's back! A dead person comes alive, or a villain comes galloping in around a corner, or a skeleton hand reaches up from the grave and grabs your throat? This was grief for me in this period, waning moments of normalcy interrupted by dramatic bouts of emotional upheaval.

I got so tired of being gripped by emotion. This is when I was scared. This is when I felt guilty for taking to my bed. This was when I needed permission, somehow, to feel these seemingly grotesque feelings of sorrow, grief, and loss.

This was when I began to find the grief groups, or they began to find me.

For that heavy and ongoing grief and fury, we need permission, allowance, witness—first and foremost from ourselves. But second, from others.

In my moody state of mourning, knowing I was couch-bound and on crutches for months, a friend connected me to an amazing woman named Angeline. She stopped by one night, late. With a young child and a lot on her plate, she was busy. This was when we made it work—and for our first encounter, I was a wreck. She tended to me, watered my wilting plants, and made me tea. I felt I could trust her and I didn't even know her. Intimate with loss herself after multiple family deaths in a row, and skilled as a chaplain, she made plans to meet me again soon in the park. She endured despite my moods, despite my punchiness, despite my lack of grace with my own pain—because she really recognized the landscape.

On weekends, Angeline and I picked up breakfast burritos and went to the park, laid out blankets under the Audobon willows, propped my bad leg on a pillow, crutches beside me, and vented about death and grieving. With her, I could be sad, but not pitied. I could be angry, but not called that. I could tell the story of my loss and she could hear me, deeply, fearlessly.

It was such a gift.

Soon, she invited me to a dinner party. I thought it was just that, but learned it was one of The Dinner Party grief groups, organized to give people space to freely speak of death and loss over casual meals. This was the remedy for the very isolation I was so sick of.

I arrived to Angeline's Dinner Party collective on a Thursday night to find four women sitting around a table, enjoying bowls of chili. Everyone was warm and kind—and they were laughing. We all just hung out. People listened to everything everyone said. Really deeply listened. It was this organic space of understanding and depth.

I just sat there and these nice women shared and asked questions, and peppered into our casual conversation were dead dads, friends, and cousins. I was surprised by how good it felt. If out in the world I was a vector of grief and mourning, trying to stuff in my pain to make everyone else more comfortable—and often failing, snapping, or lashing out—here, in this room, I was just another person. Not morbid. Not scary. Not freaky for wanting to talk about a dead parent or a dead body or a grave, but another person with a common experience of reality. And oddly, it was very fun to just be together. We didn't intentionally talk about death, we talked about everything, but death, in this room, was simply not a taboo addition to the conversation.

With this group, I could make this a year of mourning—make this a time to mourn. In this room, I could pause and grieve.

When Angeline moved to Seattle, her grief group expired, and, like clockwork, I was randomly invited to another Dinner Party grief group by a woman I waitressed with at Tryst back in 2005. This Dinner Party was on Zoom. I was again pleasantly surprised by how nourishing it felt just being able to talk about death anniversaries, gravestones, how to take time off work, what to do with haunting memories or guilt or shame or the desire to break valuables or anything else that was normal to those of us on the call. I felt the same about Modern Loss and its Facebook group; the solidarity built around the commonality of loss was deeply affirming and comforting. This was a space that could only be understood by others who had navigated the terrain. This thing I missed in so many of my relationships after the death of my father, this basic mutual understanding, here I found it.

When I felt I was supposed to stop grieving, when I felt unsupported, when I felt frustrated with the ongoing horrors of grief riddling my body, mind, and spirit, it was in part because I felt that someone somewhere was dictating: Enough is enough. Somehow, I was convinced that I was not to speak of what I was going through.

I felt I was grieving for too long. (I was not.)

I felt I was weird for still being sad. (I was not.)

I felt like a cry baby for still being floored by grief. (I was not.)

I kept coming back to the questions:

What is allowed?

What is normal?

Who decides?

And who, in our adulthood, do we give the power to decide for us?

Grief groups gave me some semblance of normalcy because we were collectively carrying such similar emotional loads, exhibiting similar grief patterns, dealing with similar subject matter. I was not alone.

I was conditioned with so many messages over the years about grief not belonging to me, grief appearing hysterical, nonsensical, like crying wolf. They had to be shed once my father died. I had to fight the urge to shut myself down. I had to internally battle for my right to feel my sadness. I had to teach myself not to judge it, and I had to seek comfort and support to make this possible.

It is not so odd to be that sad bird at a party, and it doesn't mean you are broken, or evil, or the problem kid. It means you are still dealing with profound pain. And this expectation to be up, to be joyful, to join the American musical dream number, to smile and prance—you might want to shelve it. You are not a failure if you are sad. You are not a failure if you are feeling haunted. You are not a failure if you don't want to look pretty today, or date, or dance, or run, or laugh. You are allowed to continue to mourn. Frown all you want.

Because we repress grief culturally, it can emerge in these horrific torrents and require space. And because we really aren't taught how to tend to our pain, let alone how to find time and space in our busy lives to do so, it's wise at this point, if you start tailgating another driver on the highway in revenge for the person cutting you off, to seek solace in a support group. Whatever that means to you—it doesn't have to be super formal. Maybe it's a coffee date with a couple of friends who also lost loved ones? Anything that allows you to speak of your loss and its aftereffects.

This is the time to parse out the scripts you were fed about grieving and repressing grief. About time limits and support networks. And this is the time to find what might be limiting you from getting the love, care, and nurturing you so deserve.

People are going to tell you to "move on." Someone will definitely suggest therapy in a way that makes you want to punch them instead of the wall. Someone else will tell you to "let go," and another person might suggest that "you're mourning too long."

Mourning is individual. Timing is personal. No one gets to decide, but you.

If, however, you are finding that you have drawn the blinds on the world and are low functioning, eating icing out of the container in bed while watching *The Wilds* for weeks on end, not bathing, getting fired from work, and maybe there are bugs in the trash—something that makes you feel you've gone too far—then maybe your friends are actually worried for your health and well-being.

You have to be honest with yourself: Is it time to wash the sheets?

Is it time for a grief group?

Group therapy is not just the stuff of twelve-step programs and TV rehab shows, which are great too, it is also a useful and sometimes vital tool for metabolizing hard times—and it comes in a lot of forms. It could be a church grief group, where you process with others and better learn the landscape of this rough emotional terrain. It could be a formal group through a hospital, a family services outlet, or a solo therapist's organization. They range in cost from free to $50 to much more, depending. But really, grief groups are generally not a big spending item. They are designed to help anyone and everyone through the horror of loss.

In the U.S., group psychotherapy entered mainstream practice after World War II. Used in different forms long before the 1950s, it was meant to treat those with emotional reactions to war, and it became globally popularized. Group therapy focuses on individuals as active participants in their own treatment, with the group assisting in their evolution. Trust, regular attendance, and the organic formation of group rules and boundaries are common features, and the result is often that individuals feel less alone, find space to process difficult emotions, and leave with new and vital tools for carrying their emotional load.

I suggest, when death, divorce, or any other major rupture is rattling your bones and making you feel like you are waking daily to a twisted combination of *Groundhog Day* and a Stephen King novel, that is when you get yourself to a grief group. Not because anything is wrong with you. But because it feels good—it feels really good to get support and care. Even though your pride will say, "I can do it alone!" Even though you might have been given cultural messages that therapy and grief groups are for the weak. Even though you fear being a burden to the therapist or the group itself. Despite any number of thoughts that we feed ourselves to keep us from moving forward, grief groups feel really good, are deeply healing, and will likely help you move along, move forward, and metabolize this massive experience.

Being honest with yourself about how much pain you are in and how much relief you really need, this is going to help your relationships, make you a better parent, a better worker bee, a better friend.

You can make your own group with others; you can join through any number of free locally offered groups at churches, hospitals, and elsewhere; you can contact The Dinner Party. I just highly recommend not going through this stage of the process alone. When no one is calling anymore and you still need to talk, when your friends seem sick of listening—go to a group.

A grief group meeting is a place where you get to be a wreck, get to parse out the loss, get to discuss the haunting memories or even the sensation that your beloved dead friend is in your room when you wake up. Every. Single. Morning. And those in the group won't get tired of hearing about your grief, because they have it too.

Don't hold that pain in for too long. It will ooze out eventually.

It will show up in your relationships. It will mess with your job. It will mess with your intestines. And your parenting. And everything under the sun in your pretty little life. Do your best in a way that is safe for you to stop pretending you are not in pain. Do everyone a favor, especially yourself, and honor your very own threshold of enough is enough.

This is how to navigate the wild and unpredictable expanse of explosive heart-rupturing loss: Know when to call in the bigger and badder tools.

Professional help does not mean weakness. It does not mean community failure. It does not have to mean insanity. Professional help means there may not be enough tools in the basic cultural toolkit we were given to deal with the profundity of loss. It means being realistic about where our training as human beings falls short, and where someone who knows the map of the terrain of trauma and deep sadness a little better than we do might help us navigate to the light at the end of the tunnel. In this case, that light does not lead to life after death, but to life in the here and now.

The ideal of neat, graceful, elegant containment of emotion and grief isn't always possible. This emotional suitcase is fat, spilling, just unable to contain all the contents. That's why the grief group helps. Or the grief counselor. That's why we need someone around who can help us sit on the bag to zip it up. But, more importantly, we need someone who can help us understand what to pack and what not to, what we need to hold on to, and what is needed for release.

I remember in Buddhist graduate school, how I loved joking with monks and chaplains, teasing them. For one thing, they had no ego and were amazing at taking jokes with good humor. But what I noticed with time was the magnitude of laughter that emerged from the wisest people I met, the ones who counseled others in grief, who had worked through their own depths in order to help those in need.

The release of all, or some, of these burdens may be the glittering, sparkling, blazing path to all the joy to come.

EXTRA SUPPORT: GRIEF GROUPS AND GRIEF COUNSELORS

According to hospice chaplain, spiritual and grief companion, and overall badass Ceciley Chambers of Providence, Rhode Island, "The act of grieving often feels not communal because death is separated out in this society. So being with others, sharing where you are at, and getting those knowing looks despite experiencing differences really helps. I think of grief as a 300 lb gorilla on your back. The advantage of a grief group is everyone has a gorilla on their back. And no, it doesn't make the gorilla go away, but it is really nice to be with others and their gorillas. Group gorilla play date."

Some people have more resilience and more tools to handle really awful things, and some have no tools for basic struggles. There are care options for almost anyone and everyone, with all kinds of coping skills and situations.

Step 1: Decide what kind of help you want: individual, group, etc. Also, what kind of grief are you suffering? Is this about a loss related to cancer? Is it about sexual trauma? Is it about divorce? Is it about death? Navigate accordingly. There is assistance for all kinds of woes, and help is often nearby. It is just a matter of searching, asking, and showing up.

Step 2: Assess your insurance situation, cash flow, etc. And navigate from there. There is grief support for every level of cost. Including free. Also decide what your make-it-or-break-its are: Do you need a therapist of a particular gender? Race? Religion? LGBTQ understanding? Kink friendly? Poly advocating? Specify these things for yourself before you search. You are worthy of having your deepest needs met, especially during bereavement.

Step 3: Does theology matter to you? Do you need a Zen Buddhist group or practitioner? A Christian group or practitioner? Etc.? Seek accordingly.

- In lieu of grief groups: Zen centers often have great grief-counseling offerings. Unitarian Universalist churches often do too. In addition, it is part of a hospice mandate to provide grief support to the public. The hospices in your area most likely offer public grief support groups. Even if you aren't connected to someone in hospice care at the time you are likely welcome.

- Spiritual Directors International offers grief-specific care, spiritual companions, and resources. Rabbis, priests, and chaplains also often offer free grief support.

There are infinite links, people, and places that might be of help—please, though, lead with intention, clarity, and probably tell a friend before you head into the vulnerable space of being cared for by another in your deepest time of need. Trust your gut. Know the difference between discomfort caused by challenging or touching the pain you have been avoiding, and discomfort because something or someone is unethical, violating boundaries, or operating in a way that compromises your own personal well-being on any front.

- Make a point to ask if your therapist is grief-informed and to specify a need for grief and grieving support. You can ask if they have experience working with trauma, death, or grieving. You can specify a need for grief counseling and ask for a referral. You have more power than you realize in selecting care. It can be less time consuming if you perform the search with a friend, partner, or family member.

Look online! Look for Modern Loss, call The Dinner Party, form your own club. Just do your best to access a group of others also navigating loss when feeling enormously isolated.

CHAPTER 9

BUT ACTUALLY, PRAY: SPIRITUAL PRACTICE AS LIFE PARTNER

"IF WE COULD FREE / THIS LOVE / OUR FEET WOULD BE LIGHT . . . "
—Alice Notley, *Mysteries of Small Houses*

My father was a theologically complex man. Enrolled in Orthodox religious school by secular parents who were angry at God for the murder of their families, he had a theological cacophony from the get-go. Still, he loved nature and meditation, and each morning over breakfast when I was growing up he preached the importance of praising the glory of the world. The flowers, the sun coming up, all of it.

My father was also angry at God. And the Bible.

When we went to synagogue, just the two of us, more often than not he left a prayer service red-faced, flustered, and confounded at the violence of the stories therein.

But he made us pray anyway.

Later in life when I found myself beginning (and eventually stopping) the work of becoming a rabbi, I finally understood that my father's complex anger at the Divine was actually a quest to go beyond an unchallenged belief in traditional Judaism. God had failed him, in some ways, at least the heavy-handed biblical version, so he sought something else, something he could trust. My father taught me to sink into the earth. To drop into the body, to drop into the flowers around me, to praise the glory of something he called "the universe." His faith was a collage of Judaism and 70's pop-spirituality, a mysticism that gave me permission to seek more and strive to learn more.

I wanted to pray more deeply.

I wanted the sort of prayer that binds you to the phenomenality of banana trees and blooming figs. I longed for prayers to join me with the massive ginger flowers and birds of paradise in my New Orleans yard. The flowers my father had admired with me, just before leaving this world. This type of prayer was a constant practice. My choice was to listen to silence, to put my bare feet in the dirt, and to remember that something far beyond this moment of grief is everlasting. This was my prayer. And prayer, when deep in grief, when disoriented, when exhausted from crying, brought me away from fear and closer to exuberance, to presence, to remembering that this year was just a moment on the spectrum of time, just a passageway in the scope of my winding life. Prayer could connect me to the ancient or to the innovative modern, and it, too, remapped moments, remapped time, realigned the values within and surrounding me.

Prayer grounded me in times of whirling, swirling emotional mayhem. Prayer helped me to grieve, to find rest before and after grieving, to not fear what I was going through. Prayer made solitude sweet, made being single not only bearable, but at times delectable. I was often communing with something so profound, so fulfilling, that Tinder felt like a silly distracting joke.

Prayer doesn't have to be Jewish. Nor Christian. It doesn't even have to be a prayer at all. You like noise? Music can be your prayer. You like cooking? For many, the alchemy of turning ingredients into dishes is medicinal, prayerlike, and devotional. Praying can mean grieving. Praying can mean crying. Praying can mean facing the deepest truth within you. Anything to remind us that we are bigger than this broken moment. Bigger, and smaller, queen of the world, dust of the earth. You like silence? Sit in it. Luxuriate in it. Remember that it is there.

Prayer is free. And prayer, like ritual, is your creation. Any way you choose. It can be a long session of singing in the shower, or a morning spent blasting Krishna Das, or listening to Ram Dass. It can be a George Clinton dance session or a daily yelling in the woods or chanting by the sea. Anything.

Despite a lifetime of Hebrew school, a bat mitzvah, a confirmation ceremony, and a lot of adult religious education, it took until my mid-twenties for me to really learn how to pray and, subsequently, how to grieve.

In a contemplative art class in graduate school, there were a few basic requirements of each session, one of them being a five-minute silent meditation at the onset. In those days, that didn't stop me from "having to go to the bathroom" every single time I was asked to sit still for five minutes. I couldn't do it.

Silence was loud. It made me anxious. It made my body hurt.

But then, someone mentioned they were doing a seven-day meditation retreat. A joke was made that I couldn't handle it. So, I wanted in.

I wanted to do what they said I couldn't. I was going to be in silence for twenty-four hours a day for seven days.

An amazing and patient professor took me on as a project and trained me to "cut my mind," essentially to interrupt my own thoughts and to return to silence. Our training sessions weren't silent though. They were very unconventional.

He knew that in order for me to find pause, I had to do it my way, and in the meantime, I needed to unwind the endless ticker tape in my head. He let me talk and talk and talk until I unwound stuck pieces of my mind and found silence in the shrine rooms that peppered the campus.

By December, after training and training and training, I did it. I drove up to the retreat in the Colorado mountains, where I was assigned a room, and finally, in a gorgeous space overlooking the snow-capped peaks, I sat with 150 other people in total silence.

At first, I was uncomfortable. I wiggled. I was agitated.

The guy directly behind me would glug his water dramatically.

Another sighed regularly.

I wanted to implode.

Most of my time the first few days was a fight with the silence. For most human beings, in stillness and silence, there will first be an internal struggle. I tried to quiet my mind, still my body, but was fixated on other people. On their smells. On their groans or their movements. We were stuck here, for days that felt like years, sitting on cushions in silence. I had to make peace with the water bottle sounds, the endless sighing, and nervous clicking of the teeth surrounding me. I finally let go by seeing myself in them. And then you know what happened?

I opened. I opened without warning, and it scared the shit out of me.

I had a flurry of visions and suddenly was reaching forward onto the ground and sobbing.

I had to leave the shrine room. I think this is why people resist meditation.

And you know what I was crying about? You know what the visions were?

My grandfather Morton's death in 1996. Ten years earlier. I was almost sick from grief unmourned.

This became my practice for the year to follow. Sit. Be still. Learn that silence was acceptable. Talk to myself in my head until the talking stopped. Be with nothing. Cry.

Most of us have grief, deep down, that was never moved through, touched, or even acknowledged. In seeing, labeling, and identifying my feelings, I began to understand how to familiarize myself with my interior landscape. I began to learn to navigate myself—my thoughts and emotions.

And I know for certain that if I can navigate silence and tears and chaos, with the right support and practice, so can anyone. So can you.

This is prayer. This is medicine for grief. This is witnessing our inner worlds. This is what makes time alone, living alone, loving alone, single life, life with oneself, life in solitude, life—yes—alive—yes—being a woman alone, magical, wonderful, manageable, amazing, triumphant, and exciting. This is the place where your inner worlds become the very things you get to fully, deeply, and truly delight in. This is honoring the stories we carry, no matter how heavy; this is arriving at this very moment and having the wherewithal to admit how glorious, and how horrific, it really is. There is only one of each of us, after all.

I had a lifetime of mourning I had not moved through. The same process happened in yoga classes, Pilates classes, dance classes, anything where I unlocked these calcified and repressed pieces of me and then folded over in tears. And then I resumed form. Poof. I heard a man once call this "powerful vulnerability," which to me is an inverse of machismo. This is life. This is grief. This is what lives within us and needs tending. This is a body processing mortality, violence, and loss.

I had to rewire the scripts in me in order to be with myself. I had to learn to sit with all the wildness, and suddenly I wasn't anxious. Suddenly I was calmer, able to sit still, less afraid of the movement around me. In this tunnel of relearning and redefining what was acceptable—a privilege of time, space, teachers, and practice—I gained skills that allowed me to face the scarier things in life: the deaths, the tragedies, all of it. I learned in my meditation years how to live, despite what the American script had taught me to repress. And that meant learning how to pray, to be still, and as a result, learning how to grieve.

Uncovering the wells of mourning within me was a transgressive process. It involved actually admitting I had pain. And it meant familiarizing myself with silence, with prayer, with dropping deep into the well in me that wasn't altered by the ebbs and flows of the world around me. It meant tapping into the part of me in which, when there, I could rest, curl up, and remember my own fortitude. And, it involved fortifying myself for the grief that flowed through me—that's what the meditation and teachers did for me. They taught me how to be with my true self.

I was taught somewhere not to grieve. Not to cry. Not to be "annoying" by having so many emotions. I was learning that in naming the things inside of me, I was actually coming alive. And in coming alive, I was breaking a code of silence in my own family. By finding my own way to pray, first in silence, and later in Hebrew, in song, in chanting and in dance, I was also finding my own way to honor history, and also me, as I am, in this very moment. I was thus able to release so much pain I was holding.

Prayers work.

They connect the heart to something bigger than this broken moment. They make grief easier for so many, bearable for others. They link people to hope. They drop so many people into something larger than mortality. It is comforting. Centering.

Prayer of all sorts can be our saving grace.

HOW TO PRAY

Shamatha Meditation (Appropriated Tibetan Tradition)

Close your eyes. Hand on chest. Count and listen to your breath. In, out, one. In, out, two. Count all the way to ten. If your thoughts come in, let them go. If you lose focus on breath and count, return to one. No judgment. Do this for five minutes. Get up. Have an ice cream. Meditation exists in every single tradition. Think Aryeh Kaplan, Thomas More, Rupi Kaur, Rumi—learning silence is the way for every way.

Hitbodedut (Appropriated Jewish Tradition)

Go outside. Alone. Stand by a tree. And talk. I mean it. Talk all your worries out. If you want, talk to the tree. If you want, talk to God. If you want, talk to your dead parent. If you want, talk to yourself. Just talk. All of it. Speak everything in your heart. Your love. Your anger. Talk. For at least ten minutes. Maybe stop then. Be quiet. Sit against the tree. Take a walk. Stretch. Lie on the ground. Breathe. Go back to work.

Psalms (Appropriated Judeo-Christian Tradition)

Turn to the prayer books you were raised with, or the ones you chose as an adult. Turn to structure, tradition, to the practices laid out for you already. Read a psalm a day. Let yourself be comforted by religion, if that is what comforts you. Read the Bible, the Koran, whatever it is that moves you. Study Tanya, one *pasuk* a day. You do you, piously.

Basic Kneeling Prayer (Borrowed Christian Tradition)

Give thanks. Just kneel by your bed and say for five minutes, in your head or out loud, all the things you are grateful for. Talk to whoever you want or no one. God not required. Just give thanks. Here's an example: "Thank you for opening my eyes today, for the warmth of my bed, for Alexa's rise-and-shine song choice. Thank you for the beautiful sky and the sound of the birds and for my clean clothes and how my joints move so I can walk. Thank you for my eyelids, for my nose, thank you for taste and for tea and for chocolate-covered almonds and for slippers and for bad book clubs." That's it. Just do it. Every day. Say. Thank you.

Draw

Sit with a notebook on a bench in a park. In your yard. On your front stoop. In the hallway. And just draw. For ten to thirty minutes. Draw exactly what you see, every nuance of light and dark, of bird and grass. Just draw. Throw your cell phone into the pond, or put it in a jar. Just no technology. No talking. No interruptions. Just bliss out and draw what you see. Make love to the landscape. Observe. Witness. Chill.

Write

Writing is a hugely useful tool for calming and witnessing and expressing the waves of grief. Set a timer for twenty minutes. Pick a word. Write it on the top of the page. Example: *hair*. And then write. Just write and write. Don't pick up the pen. This is the Nancy Aronie method. If you get sick of writing or have nothing to say, write "I am sick of writing. I have nothing to say. I see purple paint on the wall." Whatever. Just. Write and write and write. Consider buying *Writing from the Heart* by Nancy Aronie or *The Artist's Way* by Julia Cameron for more comprehensive guides to daily writing practices. Do this. Every day. (Or don't.) Morning or night. Be your own lover. Witness your own brilliant world.

Sing

Chant. Sing. Bellow. Mantra. Yell. Moan. Just stop thinking and use your voice and enjoy how your chest vibrates with sound. Do you. You know which of these applies. Just close your eyes and bliss out on sound. Whether it's a scale or a long steady *om*. It calms. And singing with others, whether it's harmonizing with a chorus or reciting a musical prayer with religious groups or rocking out at band practice, is a powerful source of interconnection and community building. An excellent antidote to loneliness. Learning to sing is, at its core, learning to pace your breathing; this is a great gift.

Dance and Stretch

Get in your bones. Stretching, yoga, qigong, tai chi, all of it. Moving muscles, fascia, increasing blood flow can transform our emotional landscapes. Shake the mess out of you. Blast Jamiroquai and leap around the house. Or cocoon in slow motion with Enya. Just leave your mind and your computer and transition to the timelessness of your own body in motion. Just move your limbs and breathe deeply and allow the feelings in you and the thoughts in you to take a back seat to being present in your physical body. This is a prayer, all its own, pushing you beyond the limitation of thinking.

Nature

Take a hike. Literally. Or a swim. Or lie under a tree, sit by a waterfall, meditate in an urban garden. Better yet, garden! Touch the earth. Get mud between your toes. Cultivate flowers. Keep them in the house. Touch into the temporal ebb and flow of the natural world. Life cycle. Appreciate beauty while it's there. Things don't bloom all the time. Embrace the solemnity of winter and the promise of spring.

CHAPTER 10

COMPOUNDED GRIEF: FIRE AND BRIMSTONE

"SHE WAS CLOSED UP LIKE A FIST. IT WAS HER VERY OWN MEMORY, NOT THEIRS, HER VERY OWN REAL AND TERRIBLE AND AND DARK MEMORY."
—Gayl Jones, *Corregidora*

"WHAT IS IT TO PICK UP THE PIECES AND TO LIVE IN THIS VERY PLACE OF DEVASTATION?"
—Veena Das, *Life and Words: Violence and the Descent into the Ordinary*

Come August, nine months after the death of my father, after zigzagging between my family and my own life in New Orleans, Louisiana became home. I fell in love with the bayou at sunset, with the willows in City Park, with the blooming magnolias and the way the air smelled like a Caribbean island early in the morning. I felt the ocean even though I could not see it.

And with August, came hurricane season. And in triples this year. Used to preparing for nor'easters when I lived in New England, I was an old hat at prepping for inclement weather and winds over 65 miles per hour. I knew to fill the bathtub with water, prepare non-perishables, charge extra phone chargers, and be certain flashlights had batteries.

When I lived in California, I had a similar practice preparing for earthquakes, and kept a bag by my bed with money, boots, a first aid kit, and a flashlight, ready to go in an emergency.

And so, when the hurricane warnings came in, I took cues from my neighbors, most of whom had lived on this block for almost forty-five years. A woman from my Mardi Gras krewe sent me a hurricane prep guide. I bought things online like a first aid kit, a whistle, and extra water. And then the neighbors emerged with more advice.

The sky was ominous before storms, the air still. One neighbor across the street had survived Hurricane Betsy and Hurricane Katrina. Her nerves were rattled, and she told me she was scared. I watched her pacing the block in slippers, awaiting the worst.

She wanted me, she said, to have an escape route.

I was raised on escape routes. We watched the news in my house religiously. On the nights I tried to get my dad to switch it off, he would turn to me, doing stretches on the floor while watching, and always say the same thing: "How will you know when it's time to go?" He reminded me that our family survived because my grandfather had read Hitler's *Mein Kampf*, because he knew that the worst was coming. We watched the news in our house to prepare for the worst to come. And I always knew where to go to hide, in case I had to. I was raised being prepared to run.

But New Orleans, as any old-hat New Orleanean knows, is not your average terrain.

I let my neighbor know that I had called an old friend in Ocean Springs, Mississippi, her mother offering a room on a retreat center property in Vancleave. My neighbor told me this was a terrible idea, that my escape plan was exactly in the storm's path.

Another neighbor, a former prison guard who lived two doors down, told me she escaped storms by getting a room in the French Quarter where generators kept the electricity on, and she was safe. This time I had a new plan, and I let her know I had booked a discounted hotel room in Hattiesburg, Mississippi, an hour and a half inland and North. She laughed. "Not there," she told me. "The storm is going North."

Apparently, every plan I was making was putting me in more danger.

Now, I felt scared. I felt alone. I felt confused by how people did this, and a bit self-pitying for doing this without a partner, or even a housemate. If the storm came, would anyone notice me? The news hadn't reached a national audience yet—this massive confluence of not one, but three storms aiming straight for New Orleans. No one in my life beyond this Mid-City block knew what was coming. (Yes, they did notice me. Yes, people checked on me, worried about me, offered to navigate together when the electricity went out. I was not alone. A privilege I recognized.)

I was taking cues from other people's fears. From other people's experience. Another neighbor told me to get gas, to fill my car, to be ready to go. What I noticed as we prepared, as I learned who on the block had a generator, what a good emergency plan was, how to take in my plants and anything that could turn into a projectile, was that some people were going into terrible nervous states, and others appeared fine. Some were terrified, and others were calm. Some showed fear, some hid it, some expressed it through shutting down, others through speeding up, staying in "go" mode.

Some had yesterday echoing with today, and others were not affected by the past because they did not carry the story—because they were new to New Orleans.

When I moved to New Orleans, I was terrified of what I knew of the Superdome in 2005. On arrival, I remember my chiropractor looking at me like I was crazy when I shared this fear with him. It had been fifteen years since Hurricane Katrina, and the Superdome was in use for sports, and balls, and gatherings of all kinds. In so many ways the city had moved on.

But come storm season, my friends who had lived through Katrina were rattled, nervous, hyperalert, experiencing extreme anxiety, PTSD, ready for the worst, and riddled with memories of the past. Fears of floods were the tip of their worries. Fears of being forgotten, of being rendered invisible, of being helpless, of rights being stripped, of insurance companies going AWOL—these were fortified by memories that just in their arrival were destabilizing.

I found myself empathizing with everyone I encountered.

And, I found myself missing my father.

I wanted to call him, to tell him of the mayhem. I also wanted to tell him how much these stories haunted me, echoed with stories I listened to from my own grandparents of governments forgetting them, of displacement, of finding family photos in the debris of life and holding on to them like treasures, of being labeled *refugees* in the very place they called home. I wanted my dad, but I also wanted this thing he, and only he, could offer me: the act of remembering something together, even if that something happened before I was born. I wanted to talk to someone who had my father's depth of knowledge concerning the violent history that preceded me.

I was gripped by the realization that with him, all his stories had died. With my father gone, so were the names he carried of the generation before him, as recorded in his memory, the history of my family according to his point of view, the anecdotes about the Bronx, my grandmother, how we got to America. All of it had died with him.

Who was plucked up?

Who was deported?

Who was enslaved?

I grieved during hurricane season for my neighbors and friends and their memories of a city under water, forgotten. I grieved for my absent father, and for the way many stories of our history died with him. I grieved for my own family's plight in Eastern Europe, and I grieved for what I learned of bodies left in the streets of New Orleans, as if a government had no obligation to pay homage to these people who worked, lived, and served this city. I grieved that horrific history was being repeated in many new ways for so many, right here, right now.

You have your own story. You may have your own daily battles with microaggressions that echo history. You, most likely, have your own heavy past that makes this present moment louder, harder, more complicated.

My cousin and I, both children and grandchildren of Holocaust survivors, have conversations about grief regularly, parsing out the stories we carry. We often look at the difference between grieving, actually moving the anger and sadness and fury through, actually having and making space to cry, actually speaking of feelings, of history, of bodies aching—the act of really processing grief, instead of allowing grief to become a mere figure, a golden calf of sorts. When grief unmourned is the inheritance from the past it can block all light from shining through.

The New York Association for New Immigrants: Hebrew Immigrant Aid Society Report 1951 record of my father and his family's arrival to New York recorded my grandparents' ability to assimilate, arrive, find healthcare and work. They recorded how dedicated and on time my family was when it came to appointments.

They, like post-Katrina insurance reports, have no record of what occurred at home at this time. There is no account of how often grandmothers cried, whether they were hopeful or angry, scorned or excited. There is no record of the discrimination they faced, or of their difficulty letting go of one language in exchange for the other. There is no record of the potential squalor of their conditions, nor the state of their lives before disaster struck, nor of how many family members they lost, whether they witnessed death and murder, the death of children, miscarriages, forced abortions, nor how long they spent in Displaced Persons camps.

There is no record of grief, how much had been passed, how much still swam in their stomachs. The agency did not record family members murdered.

Pain that was too large to mend, or to feel, or to address, issues that needed healing were often left untended. I like to joke about how when my grandparents came to America on a boat in 1950, war refugees with false papers, when they started their lives in the Bronx with $30 total, they weren't like, "Gosh, I feel really stressed because my sisters, brothers, mother, father, cousins, baker, teacher, butcher, were killed, maybe I need a hot stone massage and a latte." They didn't have time to rest, nor money for spa treatments, nor resources for trauma healing.

There was no time, nor space, to mourn and process all that was lost.

For so many, this remains the case.

A lot of people experience grief, and then more grief, and then even more grief, with no relief. Loss, for so many, is not just about the one occurring in this moment, but the many that preceded this moment, the many losses never mourned, never properly grieved, never given space or time or resources to be grieved, never laid to rest. This loss, plus losses from the past, may be aggravated by other deaths, other crimes, other blows to the nervous system, sometimes daily.

This is compounded grief.

When grief sits on grief and more grief. Horror on horror, past and present, can leave people emotionally destabilized, highly anxious, and steadily unnerved. Especially when the horrors experienced are ignored, racially motivated in current time, not just past, played down, erased by the society you live in and then repeated in new forms.

To have the space to speak of pain is a privilege, because those able to talk about it are the very people who can. This is the time, this moment of grief in layers, to acknowledge history, to acknowledge the current moment, and to acknowledge recent losses.

What you remember is real.

Compounded grief can be complicated by the grief and loss and trauma many inherit just by being born. From histories of deportation, slavery, murder, and genocide to more recent accidents, losses, and events. The losses of parents and grandparents can live in the body, psyche, and can embed within cultural messages. And worse, some of these histories are echoed in current events, repeated, riddling and rattling the nervous systems, inciting fear, and bringing on an almost completely unmanageable torrent of negative feelings.

Now is the time to track the symptoms that persist, or double and triple up, and write them all down. Now is the time to take a litmus test of whether this grief is about something new, or something ancient. The hope is to not let things grow too far out of control, to not harm the self or others.

Some ways that past traumas, losses, deaths, genocides, wars, murders, and other horrors might show up in the present moment, especially for those experiencing ongoing forms of oppression:

- Paranoia.
- Stomach issues.
- Spontaneous crying.

- Sciatica and ruptured disks.
- Narcissism.
- Erratic eating habits.
- Love as violence.
- Power as love.
- Bed wetting.
- Seizures.
- Severe body pain with no warning.
- Yelling sporadically.
- Blanking out.
- Forgetting things.
- Scratching uncontrollably.
- Pulling out hair.

Acute grief, a reference to something akin to that week I watched my father die and I was unable to function and was in extreme emotional hormonal nervous system takeover, may be recurring for some. *Complicated grief* can often be a neutering term for something called *ongoing grief*, a grief that lingers—one might call the results of ongoing grief *melancholia* or *depression*. This is *unresolved grief*, or a sadness stuck in the body or too horrific to feel through. There's also *disenfranchised grief*, aka gaslighting, a grief one may experience that is played down or not recognized or acknowledged by others or by the society in which they live.

And then there is *compounded grief*, when layers and horrors pile up in your life, when the feelings are hard to differentiate, when coming up for air never provides quite enough oxygen.

Grief for so many is not about a singular loss.

Shit will happen before people have time to heal. This is the I-thought-it-would-be-getting-a-bit-easier stage, and if it's not, this is the oh-my-goodness-it-is-getting-worse stage, the something-new-and-maybe-old-is-wrong stage, the this-might-be-about-something-much-bigger-than-this-moment grief.

As a single woman who might be able to huddle away from the public eye and hide this pain, it is vital to admit the factors at play, to seek witness in community, in family or friends or whatever support can help you to admit the stories surging through you: stories from the past, the recent past, and the present. Especially as a single woman who might be culturally tasked with caring for others, endlessly, before caring for herself.

These concerns are legitimate. The past is real. As is this moment.

What ails you is real.

Part of inheriting trauma can be to normalize suffering, to act like it's just fine to live with severe anxiety and pain. Notice these otherwise accepted elements of life, mark them as pivot points, places where grief needs tending, and wounds need healing. Even if that tending and healing can't come for a decade or even a lifetime, the act of labeling history and harm is a step in the right direction.

When symptoms arise out of the blue, when history gets loud, this is a simple time to admit the past is not yet laid to rest, especially when a story erased is real, and has real impacts on this lived moment.

It is said that those who heal their generation heal seven generations back and seven generations forward. Begin with writing the story down, begin with seeing how heavy this load may be.

Begin with you.

STABILIZING YOUR NERVOUS SYSTEM IN A PINCH

In times of repeated griefs, compounded horrors, traumas, acts of violence, and hate, it is likely that you will experience full nervous system overload, shut down, and beyond. Compounded grief, inherited trauma, and loss squared, when they rumble in, sometimes require emergency mitigation.

How might one stabilize the nervous system when they can't contact a mental health professional?

Youth trauma counselor Chlöe Berlin's suggestions for nervous system stasis:

Body-Based Practices:
- Progressive Muscle Relaxation. Tightening, holding, and releasing every muscle, slowly, from your head down to your toes.

- Dramatic temperature changes can make escalated moments more bearable.

- Submerging one's face in a bowl of ice water for ten-second increments, then taking it out for ten seconds, six times each, is a two-minute panic attack cure. It stimulates the vagus nerve and literally slows your heart rate.

- There are also less drastic ways to incorporate temperature into your stabilizing practice. Take a cold shower. Place ice cubes on your pressure points. Hold a warm drink to your face and let the steam soften your skin. Use a heating pad. Keep oranges in the freezer for a tactile and aromatic fidget toy.

- Brief bouts of cardio exercise can help if you feel that you are about to start hyperventilating (but not while you are actively hyperventilating). Give me twenty jumping jacks. A dozen sit-ups. This is simply because the nature of high-intensity exercise forces your body to regulate breath in a more intuitive way.

- Use rhythmic movement to channel your emotions. Dancing, drumming, and tantric beats all aid the restructuring of a traumatized brain.

Mental Practices:
- In the heat of the moment, sometimes distraction is the best you can do. Count backwards from 100. Name all of the sounds you can hear. All of the colors you can see. This is a temporary fix for a moment of dysregulation.

- Prioritizing one task ("one thing at a time") instead of trying to multitask. Place an extra emphasis on completing a single task. Encouraging one to finish a simple project and even a basic errand might sound silly, but it helps to provide a grieving person with a sense of control, order, and achievement. (Art projects, craft projects, writing letters, making altars, collages, Mardi Gras costumes, all of it.)

- Integrate imagery/visualization into your meditation practice. Visual aids are grounding for people whose heightened nervous system responses leave them feeling discombobulated.

- Lean into consistent, long-term relationships. (Good for all who can find them—don't need to be marital. Can be friends, therapists, grandmothers, clergy.) It also doesn't need to be so intimate. It could be a postal worker you see each morning, or a neighbor at the dog park. But take time to appreciate and experience steady and long-term connections.

- Work to accept emotions before trying to change them.

- Listen to music that matches and/or shifts your mood.

PART III

THE FUTURE

"WOMEN AMAZE ME."

—Bobbie Louise Hawkins, *Absolutely Eden*

CHAPTER 11

FORGET CAKE, MAKE RITUALS: MEMORIALIZING ON YOUR TERMS

"USE YOUR IMAGINATION—RECREATE AMONG DYING TREES STUCK IN CRACKED SILT THE SHAPES OF DEAD AND GONE THINGS: ETCH CLAWS AND FINS AND SCALES INTO EARTH, CUT THE SKY INTO WINGS—AGITATE STILLNESS."
—Laura Mullen, *Enduring Freedom* ("Bride of the Bayou")

"ANY RITUAL IS AN OPPORTUNITY FOR TRANSFORMATION. TO DO RITUAL, YOU MUST BE WILLING TO BE TRANSFORMED IN SOME WAY."
—Starhawk, *Truth or Dare: Encounters with Power, Authority, and Mystery*

My father was really strict about who was and was not allowed to say the Mourner's *Kaddish*, the Jewish prayer for the dead. This prayer is to be said for eleven months following the burial of an immediate family member, traditionally three times daily during prayer services, and the mourner rises while the others bear witness and support them. The words are not what you might expect: they proclaim the magnificence and glory of the Divine, over and over again. As they rise to say the prayer for their dead, mourners are witnessed by a community of a minimum of ten people, a *minyan*.

The idea is to keep the mourner, who is usually fixated on death and graves and what is absent, focused instead on love, life, the heights of the Divine on high, on the most beautiful. In some ways it is a free therapy practice—a group support team reminding the griever not to forget their loss, and at the same time, not to forget the good in the world. And as their ability to do so waxes and wanes, they return to this practice, for a year, hammering it in to not forget, in this case, God. Or, as I interpret it, the power of community, of witness, and of stating positive intentions in times of deep distress.

Kaddish, most importantly, cannot be cited alone.

So many who go through loss end up suddenly alone. These old rituals are designed for people who lose a spouse or a parent or someone who keeps a home full, warm, alive. These old rituals are meant to comfort the single person, the alone person, to bring them into communal love and care and to help them be seen in their time of loss, to help them admit in the throes of devastation that this pain they are feeling is real, that this dead person is gone, and most importantly, that the living are still alive. And they give us something to touch, to move, a way to find a sense of agency in a time of so much overwhelm.

Kaddish is a daily reminder of this very thing: that the living are still alive, that life and love and beauty, despite the deep shroud of pain and absence death will wrap us in, persevere.

Beside my father in synagogue as a child, I tried to rise and stand for the dead when someone was killed by the police, or when my friends lost their parents, or when any other bad thing happened. In these moments, I wanted to stand for people not traditionally included in the call to rise for *Kaddish*—people outside the immediate family. And my father, who was thrust into ultrareligious *Lubavitch yeshiva* as a child in the Bronx, was a stickler for following rules—especially when it came to honoring the dead. He wanted grief parsed out. He wanted certain losses guarded. He wanted to draw lines around who was and was not allowed to mourn. And he would always insist that I sit down.

"Those prayers are for people who lost their parents, their children, their spouse, not for you," he would chastise. I felt ashamed, and frustrated, and sat down.

I remember, however, many years later, all of us on my father's side, gathering in Paramus, New Jersey, for the burial of my majestic great aunt Rajna. She attended an Orthodox gender-divided synagogue, and at her burial, when the time came, there were not ten men. A *minyan* needs to be ten people, and in old school tradition, those ten need to be cisgender men. We were mostly women, and the rabbi refused to say *Kaddish*. I remember looking at my father and something strange and profound passing between us as he nodded, indicating that he gave me permission to speak up.

"We are okay," I said on behalf of my family, with my father's consent, "with having women say *Kaddish*. They count for this moment. We want to say *Kaddish*." And the rabbi was kind and stepped back as I and ten relatives of mixed genders recited *Kaddish* for the last Holocaust survivor in our family. A transitioning moment from past to future.

When my father died, it was my formal turn at reciting *Kaddish*. I was finally allowed, according to formal Jewish law, to stand. I had lost an immediate family member, a parent, and was expected to stand every single day at a *minyan*, saying the formal *Kaddish* on his behalf, for eleven months after his passing. I knew how much it meant to him—and in so many ways to me—to practice and enact this ritual.

Despite New Orleans having a large Jewish community, and a lot of synagogues, a daily *minyan* is generally hard to come by in a smaller community, especially in less orthodox iterations. The daily call to prayer was honored still by the ultra-Orthodox, Chabad-Lubavitch movement, that same strict sect my father was educated by as a kid, one that mandates gender-divided prayer.

When I couldn't find a service in my sect of Judaism to attend daily—I tried one with Chabad. It was thirteen black-hat *Chassidic* men and me, alone on one side of a room divider. If this was meant to comfort me, bring me closer to a belief in the Divine, allow me to find community in my time of loss, it failed. I felt deeply alone and also rubbed at being forced to separate by gender—something I respect for others—but was bothered by deeply as I stood alone reciting the prayer for my dead father. It just did not feel right.

I felt guilty for not saying *Kaddish* in person with a group of ten people daily. For this mandated daily prayer for the dead that I was determined to follow, to say, to make into an honoring of both my father's life and my own grief, I was going to have to improvise. Even with my innovative individual practices, I was still cursed with this ongoing fear: Was I a bad griever? When this fear arose, instead of lying in bed and hating myself for not being a better Jew, I made my own group rituals. I knew for my father, as I imagined him, this was good, and I knew for me, in my grief, I needed more communal witness as I navigated loss alone.

This is the time for ritual.

This is the time for making it up.

For so long in my family, mourning was guarded and tiered—it was marked who could mourn and when. The relatives who had lived through war often balked at the mundane concerns of my generation. "Suffer?" my great uncle with his Auschwitz tattoo on his wrist used to say when I complained, "You think you suffer? Suffer! Let me tell you, suffer is to be a slave in a labor camp. Suffer is to be starved." And still, what I learned, over time, was that I was carrying grief for family members still scarred by the past. I was an empath, and I needed a ritual practice, a ritual for grieving different from the formal one allotted by religious law.

In order to release all I had been trained to hold deep inside, I had to bypass my father's rules for when to mourn; when to stand for the dead; and how, when, and why to use ancient Jewish rituals in the modern context. I had to learn to grieve despite being told how, when, and why. I learned how to listen to myself and build my own rituals for grieving when tradition didn't allow for the honoring of the feelings and experiences I was living.

I took my cues for making my own grief rituals from the ancient, from my father's strict laws, and I went with it. I gleaned the following from the model of *Kaddish* before leaping into creative ritual practice:

1. There's a use to parsing out the difference between acute and peripheral losses. All can be honored, but those in acute states are truly experiencing something that requires a particular tending, attending, and caring for. Can both be honored at once? Could I somehow honor collective and individual loss at once?

2. Community witness and practice is vital. *Kaddish* in its particularities serves in helping people come to terms with the truth of loss, to find acceptance of this truth, and to bring closure. It gives a really solid framework to follow when you cannot think—you just do this thing. And it surrounds the suffering person in a daily community that they don't need to organize or think about. They just show up.

3. Make your own version as needed. And implement it as regular ritual to hold space for loss, especially when you are low functioning, when you can't rise, when you hate the earth you stand on for taking away your loved one and subsuming them six feet under (or wherever your person went). These daily practices are designed for the support of the living, for the honoring of the dead, and for the building of community in times of distress. Can you invent your own?

4. When feeling guilty for not being religious enough, strict enough, correct according to the finger-shaking condemnation of a religious parent—when

unable to do the rituals as taught to you—always remember, in the wise words of Community Leader Rachel Rudman: "You are honoring the dead—not in that very traditional way—but in very good ways." Again, these creative practices are individual, community, and ritual support for when we cannot easily function. You do you.

When I knew I couldn't do *Kaddish* the traditional way, and when I knew my father's death was permeating every moment of my days in the months after he died, I began to take an inventory of my options. One friend, whom I met in Vermont after she lost her mother, told me that instead of saying *Kaddish* daily, she translated a line of Italian poetry every day for a year in honor of her mother. Another friend, who lost her love, gifted me paper white bulbs that she planted annually and watched bloom around the time of his death. My sister-in-law organized her own weekly service and took the time to remember her father, and my sister adopted the same, doing a weekly *Kaddish* online. Taking cues from those I learned from in years past, I felt emboldened to do things my way.

My rituals began small. In the first months without my father, small elements around my house kept him near. I ordered my father's weird selection of favorite groceries. I got dark chocolate and large bowls of cherries. Then I started making loose leaf tea every morning, like he did. I propped a photo of him in the kitchen near some flowers and lit a candle when I woke up, burned palo santo or sage, something that made it feel like I was protecting or honoring his spirit. I kept his hat in my office. I slept in his T-shirts and sweaters—a practice that, with time, became too much. (With time, every practice shifted and changed according to where I was in my grieving process. The truth is, it did get easier, and then my need to cling to my father's life waned.) I made a book of photos of just us and kept it on my coffee table.

Burning incense, praying to my ancestors, imagining my father in the room, buying a hat to emblematically replica his style were other small and simple practices that gave me agency over my own experience of loss. They allowed me to incorporate elements of my father into this new reality of one-year-later without him. I gathered people for prayer, I hosted nights to remember my father in front of friends, and I collected images memorializing our relationship (for example, our Facetime screenshots), trying to capture our unique and boisterous way of relating. I was so worried about forgetting him; it felt nice to tangibly hold on to elements of us, of him, of my dad.

It was in this way that I was able to accept this strange reality of mortality as a piece of being alive—not a tragedy, not an aberration, but a thing everyone will go through, a thing we are marked with.

Everyone has their rituals. Some learned, some self-taught. Acting out our feelings in tangible ways, making celebrations and ceremonies, creating visual manifestations of our inner worlds: This is our right. And one that is often bypassed by the cultural, religious, and communal systems of thought and practice that guided us to this moment. You don't need frankincense and myrrh, or a formal *minyan*, or a sacrament to make your own meaning or structure for guiding yourself through your losses. There are rituals for anything and everything—for miscarriages, for divorces, for clearing the residue of rape.

Pick your own ritual. Your own practice. Follow a religious code, or make one up.

Find a ritual that makes you feel comforted.

A close friend threw an "Independence Day Party" after her divorce. She and her friends dressed in torn bridesmaids dresses and shared the lessons they'd learned by leaving men who had cheated on them or abused them. This self-made ritual was what she held on to. This moment that allowed her to transition from one point in her life to the next by marking time with practice, visual ritual, and celebration. Ritual exploration can be the needle that sews the seams of our lives and allows us to hold on, let go, and move forward, all at once.

What ritual offers is a demarcated measurement of time after a moment of great loss. *Kaddish* offered me a new marker of time—one that began with the death of my father.

Anniversaries, birthdays, death days, and other pre-marked moments in time can feel brutal in how they remind us that the dead are still dead. Still gone. That life has continued on without them. However, anniversaries of this kind are also excellent markers for making rituals, for marking the progression of time in this new phase of life—a life after loss. While traditionally I was taught to mark a year from my father's death, called a *yahrzeit*, as the formal anniversary marker, I needed and wanted rituals sooner—so I made them.

I began marking important days, giving my loss a calendar of its own. First was June 4, the weekend of my father and my one-year anniversary visiting New Orleans together, and the one and only time he saw my home here. I lamented, early in his sickness, not being able to share a cappuccino with him at Angelo Brocato, but on this anniversary I marked it with meaning by having a biscotti and a coffee there. I toasted my father.

What may seem like silly actions offered me ways to take my interior loss and externalize it into an actionable ritual.

Next came Father's Day, and then, soon thereafter on June 19th, my father's birthday. I spent Father's Day with Savanah, who also lost her father that year. We were both marked by a recent loss, so we were free to say anything morbid or frightening to those of our friends terrified of the very parental loss we were coping with. To celebrate our fathers and their joy, we drove across the causeway, through bayou and lake regions, blasting music and picking up baked goods in New Orleans East at Dong Phuong.

To mark the six months since his passing and the one-year mark, I had Zoom gatherings with friends far and near, and we remembered the joyful exuberance of my father, together. For the other days when the memories might come calling, I try to build in a dinner with a friend, someone to whom I can speak about my memories and my grief.

Being witnessed is an act of ritual. Whether there be one or two or ten or 200 people, to have a witness, a mirror, your own voice on a recorder, a friend holding your hand over a good meal of fried chicken, that witness marks time. We want to build in as many ways to metabolize this truth: loss has marked our lives. The more witness, the more the shock wears off and we can come to terms with the unfathomable reality of the change that took place.

And witness does not require partnership nor marriage nor a lover. You can sleep alone, spread-eagle in your bed and still find witness. I promise.

When I can't find the exact person I want to be vulnerable with I have a few choices:

1. Choose a new friend and tell them the truth, don't drown them in it, but one or two sentences can be magical heart openers. "Hey, I don't want to be a huge burden, I know we are all going through it, but it's the anniversary of my father's terminal diagnosis and I would love some company. Want to have dinner?"
2. Make a Zoom or Facetime call with family, chosen or otherwise.
3. Make a special occasion alone—drive to the beach, go to dinner, or fold into a movie. These solo meaningful days have been incredibly powerful for me.
4. Watching television can be a major tool in grief—witnessing other people's losses and crying alone with the TV's emotional safety net for protection. Never, ever underestimate the power of television to help move grief through. My father, I will say, would have hated this. He detested the trashy TV I watched, and often grew nearly enraged at the sight of me watching

TV during the day. But when I had the time, and when I grieved, I learned that television was also my wailer, my accompaniment, the provocateur that would usher the flow of tears I so needed. I learned to cling to onscreen narratives that pushed the emotions through me, mirrored my insides, and helped me cultivate an understanding of my emotional state. And so, provoked by the onscreen burial of a fancy country singer mom on *Nashville*, and a very emo dad on *This Is Us*, I cried. I cried for me. I cried with Kevin, Randall, and Kate. And with Maddie, Daphne, and Deacon. I grieved.

It's also a good idea to have a "human contact plan" on big memorial days—especially if you live alone. For example, on the six-month anniversary of my father's death, which felt potent to me, I asked for a Zoom gathering of friends who knew him. We all remembered him, together. It felt special, even though it didn't go at all as planned. Not as many people wanted to share their memories as I had hoped, and at times it felt that people were more excited to catch up with one another than to honor my dad. So, it wasn't perfect—but it was exactly what I needed. It not only comforted me to see my friends, but the imperfection of it all gave me the fuel to cry later that evening. It was an experience to hold on to.

What I found was that people wanted to participate in my rituals. People wanted to be part of the process of honoring, of remembering, of comforting. Rituals built community. Brené Brown says it's really important to go to funerals. As important as it is to go to weddings. And I agree.

These moments of vulnerable loss, these moments of sharing comfort and sharing mourning, they create intimacy. They solidify connections. They forge new relationships and they strengthen old ones. Death and loss are times where love, when shown, lands deeply.

Yes. Rituals build community. They did for me, and they will for you.

And, things will go wrong. People will say the wrong things. You will plan the best event on earth and three people will come drunk. Someone's kid will poop in the yard. Or you will expect to be sad, but won't be, or vice versa.

Perhaps on a death-a-versary you'll feel nothing, but the absence of your loved one on your own birthday may wreck you. There is no rhyme or reason to when grief will arrive, but I would say: when in doubt, have a small plan to do something to mark the day. Take cues from your spiritual or religious tradition if you want, but really, take your cues from deep in your heart and also from the needs of fellow mourners.

Does your family need something? Be the ritual provider. Give them something to touch and see and share their feelings in tangible ways. It will make all the difference—to all of you.

I was asked to lead a grieving ritual for fifty people at the Peristyle at City Park one evening. Surrounded peripherally by a classic New Orleans boisterous mix of picnickers, dance troupes, and small private costume parties, we were a group gathering for Friday-night prayer. I copied an online ritual put in place by a collective of spiritual colleagues, citing their way of delineating tiers of immediate intimate loss to collective grief. "We have all known death this year," I said. "Please stand and say the name of anyone you lost in the past week who is a close friend or family member. The past six weeks. The past six months. The past year." People stood for grandmothers and cousins and friends, for whole communities, and for things they had heard about on the news.

Suddenly every single person was standing. And when it was time to say the prayer for the dead, I expected them to join, for us all to say it together.

But I was the only one who lost a parent that year.

I was the only one.

And despite being a nontraditional gathering that usually says *Kaddish* together, for some reason they were all silent. They all witnessed me as I spoke the words. Alone. And in that moment I was held in witness so profound that for a brief moment I saw my grief, my father gone.

I sat down stunned, surprisingly emotional. The ritual I was meant to lead for others ended up feeding me what I needed most in that moment. I was seen in my time of mourning.

Ritual as medicine works.

In Jewish tradition, the mourner who lost a parent stops saying *Kaddish* eleven months after the burial, leaving a one-month period to adjust to that new reality, before the next ritual. This month is the transition to closure of the year of mourning. I was shocked by how impactful and effective these time markers and ritual practices were in helping me understand and metabolize my grief, and also in giving me permission to let it go.

When I stopped saying *Kaddish* at eleven months, it was an adjustment. It meant I was no longer the primary mourner, no longer standing and witnessed. When I stopped saying *Kaddish*, I was transitioning, during that prayer, from standing to sitting, from being witnessed to holding space for other mourners. At eleven months I became the support, not the supported.

All my smaller rituals culminated in this last month—the pause between *Kaddish* completed at eleven months and the final graveside ritual at twelve months. This eleven-months mark was a threshold I crossed, a transitioning out of my acute time of loss and into rejoining the living. I was surprised at how profoundly different I felt on the other side, as if a portal to my grief—which was still present but gentler—had suddenly closed. And not all at once, not on the clock I had expected, but on the far side of all of these rituals I could look back at time before and time after, and see all the differences.

It gave me so much strength to see that map.

Between the eleven months when *Kaddish* ceases and the one-year mark is a season of adjustment. This one month is similar to that first walkabout after week one—it is a transition period from cocooning inward to facing the world again, in full. This is not to say mourning is over, or going to end. I am not sure mourning ever ends. But the sense of being marked by death, of walking through the world with part of me linked to the grave, this began, in this time, to wither away.

I chose not to cut my hair for the duration of the eleven months of mourning. There are Jewish mourning rituals for men around not shaving or cutting hair, and I wanted my own version. It felt profound, as my hair grew, knowing what it carried—a year of mourning. And then, a few days after *Kaddish* ended, I allowed myself to go to a salon, to get a haircut, and to dye my dark brown hair light pink.

Silly as it may sound, visual markers of change made all the difference. I could see and feel a change in me—I had been through something life altering. I wanted something to show for it.

That space of the lead up to the one-year anniversary, for me, was completely new territory. Big death-a-versaries require bigger bolstering. The landscape of emotions can be unpredictable. I was worried that I had used up all of my resources in the past year. I was scared to ask for more support during the one-year ritual.

I felt I had cashed in on all my support chips. (I hadn't.)

I felt guilty for wanting or needing anyone to Zoom me, ever again. (Nobody minded at all.)

I had written, I decided, one too many emails asking for support. (It wasn't true.)

When I realized the magnitude of this anniversary, I got over myself and gathered a group in my yard in New Orleans before flying to be with my family. A rabbi friend offered to do a small ceremony. My neighbor Jim helped me string lights so we could see in the dark. People from my Mardi Gras krewe came. Jewish community friends came. Work colleagues came. I felt grateful and vulnerable. The ceremony was quiet, intimate, prayerful. People listened as I spoke about who my father was. This was my first private ritual closing a year of mourning.

In the Jewish tradition, the last time-bound ritual for the year of mourning a parent is the gravestone unveiling. Up until this point, the grave, dug so quickly, is left without a stone. This last marking of ritual closed my year of mourning.

It took moving through this cycle to truly understand the deep power of these practices.

ANNIVERSARIES

- **Define these for yourself.** Birthdays? Death days? What days (or weeks or seasons . . .) of memory are intense for you? Be prepared to get this wrong. But trying is always a good idea.

- **Make space to tell your loved one's story.** To friends. In an essay. In an obituary. In a photo montage. In a play. In whatever way—tell the story. So you don't have to hold it so tight.

- **Remember that rituals are markers of transformation moments** and transitions and can be used for any and every moment of change, of shift, of moving from one point to another.

A Few Ideas:

- **A ritual to show you are mourning**—not shaving, not cutting hair, something different from your norm.

- **Birthdays of the dead.** Death days. Days of importance in your own family.

- **Time bound markers**—one month, six months, one year, etc. By acting and doing things on these days, I was able to see and move my grief, rather than be controlled by it.

- **Anything else that feels like a meaningful or challenging day for you**—build ritual into it; allow yourself to honor the gray zone, to fold in the crease, to build a bridge from past to future.

- **Mark your calendar.** Notify people you want to participate. You are allowed to do this. You are allowed to create meaning. This is your life. Set up a support system in advance.

- **Assess basic needs.** Devise a plan to meet them. Forward planning for hard days makes all the difference.

- **Know you might fail.** Let it go, knowing it will be something good, and something bad, and that inevitably, no matter how sweet the day, the loss will still be there, wagging its pesky little tail.

HOW TO BUILD A RITUAL

Holistic Medicine Healer, Malka Lew, on How to Build a Ritual:

- **Why rituals?** Rituals offer tangible ways to make meaning, build community, and to engage with grief. Ancient information is often hidden because of trauma and war, and there's a lot of use in engaging old ways. We need wisdom from ancient cultures now more than ever.

- **What is a ritual?** A ritual just marks going from one space to another—entering a different space. Whatever happens in a ritual it can be useful to offer a marking from one thing to another. An opening and a closing of that ritual can serve to mark the edges of this experience.

- **What does sacred mean?** Sacred means connected with life. Awake and connected to the presence of love in life and death. Love is something that is always present but not always recognized—a benevolent force, grace and care.

- **A ritual means, then, to make something sacred.** So find some kind of way you make it sacred: your clothes, your words, your objects—decoration, flowers— make the space beautiful, however you can make that moment sacred to you.

- **A ritual is set in motion with intention-setting.** Speak intentions. Write intentions. Whisper intentions. In a group ritual, collective and individual intentions can be set or listened to.

- **Marking the transition to the sacred.** I would offer up meaningful words, be they prayers or mantras or just a simple statement of intention and gratitude before you begin and in whatever way you are transitioning into a sacred space.

- **Most vital, consider marking an opening and a closing.** An opening—something to signify entering space or beginning ritual—a song, a candle, a spoken incantation to the sacred space and a closing down of it. Maybe everyone puts their prayer into a candle and sets it somewhere, and the ending is the way of listening to the message. A marking when it begins and when you leave.

- **Communal protection is honoring the land.** To honor the land you are on and the ancestors of that land. To recognize them is important to any ritual. Bring your protection—protection means to honor what is there.

- **Altars for grieving.** How I connect and build a ritual is first of all how I can connect with building an altar for that person. The tangible and visible process of building an altar is personal.

  - **Where?** How and where you feel connected to them, build it there, in your home, wherever you feel.

  - **What?** Marking a place with an object—elements of the person or experience gone—a picture, something that evokes your memories.

  - **Elements.** To represent the four elements you can bring in rocks or crystals to represent earth elements; you can bring in a feather for air, a candle for fire, and provide some water. All the elements there help to remind us we are part of a much bigger picture.

  - **How?** You can sit in silence, or you can state an invocation, an intention. If moved, then you can begin to talk to the person gone. Pray to them and speak and continue to, and have that conversation in whatever way that you feel—from your heart.

  - **Closing the altar.** After you are done talking, you can sit for a moment and just meditate and listen to whatever messages are coming to you.

CHAPTER 12

IF THERE'S SUCH A THING AS "COMPLETED GRIEF," THIS IS IT

"HERE IN THE SHADOW OF THE EMPIRE STATE BUILDING, DEATH AND THE GRAVEYARD ARE FINAL."

—Zora Neale Hurston, *Tell My Horse*

The first time I saw my father's gravesite was a year earlier, at his burial, four days after he died. It was twenty degrees out. I wore booties—thin leather moccasins that my cousin and I decided were the right boots for the weather. We were very wrong. The shoes quickly soaked through with snow, and the ground itself was ice cold. Soon my feet began to freeze.

I don't remember being very sad as we buried my father. I remember hopping about. I remember standing on a collapsed folding chair to buffer against the frozen earth I stood upon. My feet were so cold they burned. As the rabbi spoke, I was not in my head or my heart but in my feet, stomping and wiggling and frozen.

That said, I do believe my cold feet gave me strength.

I was able to help direct the burial, to advocate for our family—rather than the cemetery workers—to be the ones to fill in the grave.

It is Jewish tradition to ceremonially toss a stone or to shovel some dirt onto the casket once it has been lowered into the grave. It's usually a thin layer, and then the family leaves and the cemetery staff fills in the grave. In recent years, though, when

Holocaust survivor relatives passed, and when they were the last ones in our family line of witnesses to what came before us, my family took to burying our own dead.

The shoveling became not a single line and a thin layer of dirt on the casket, but a long, slow, familial dedication to honoring our people. In rotation, the strongest of the family would continue to shovel the dirt. We sang *Ozi V'zimrat Yah*, this time on repeat for a half hour, and we went around—Sol, David, Ruthie, me, Daniela, Calvin, Ariel, Sam—and we filled the grave until leveled. So many of our predecessors were buried in unmarked mass graves. So many bones were mangled and left unrecognized in my family line.

Graveyards and gravestones in my family are markers of dignity, of humanity, of recognition, of tradition, and even in death, a marker of survival. My father's parents are buried in an enormous Jewish cemetery in Paramus, New Jersey, in a site dedicated to all who survived the death sweeps of their small town in Zamość, Poland. At each burial over the years—for my great aunt Rajna; her husband, David; my great-uncle Moishe; my grandma Paula; my grandpa Morton; and all the others I am not naming—we buried one but remembered all. For my family, grief was never a singular act.

And not only did I see and say hello to this garden of our family's dead, but surrounding them were other survivors from Zamość, not family, but also marking the survival and, simultaneously, the murderous end of an enormous community. There's a trail of loss that can't be contained in my family lineage.

This full burial, by the hands of family members and not strangers, at my father's burial, was an act of love. An act of reclamation and dignity. This ritual act of closure freed us to move on with personal dignity.

My first trip back to the cemetery was made alone, over the summer, about eight months after my father's death. My mother wanted me to visit the grave with her. I wasn't ready.

My mother and I had spent long stretches of time together in the year after my father's death. We were difficult roommates: two grievers, two people wrestling with different memories, different histories and relationships to the same dead man. She told me she had already been to the grave a few times. She left stones. Spoke to him at length about the state of the world.

Me? I just didn't want to go.

Even though buried, he was everywhere. His things in the house, his habits, his favorite tree, his favorite store, his favorite art gallery. Strangers in stores, realizing who I was, told me my dad was crazy and wonderful, that they called him "Padrino." When I got in his car, it was filled with trash from when he was alive. That trash was so grotesque to me—somehow made my father's absence wholly irrational. He was just here. This is his mess. Where the fuck is my dad?

I procrastinated. I would drive through town the very longest ways to avoid the cemetery.

When I finally went the first time, it was quick, in and out. I drove up to the graveyard, walked by his grave, was very matter-of-fact. "Yup," I said to myself, "there he is." I drove away. I was still not ready yet to take this in.

And then, another time, it hit me in a wave when I pulled up to the cemetery. "Dad," I almost yelled, "what are you doing down there?" I was being funny and angry—I wanted to dig him up—I wanted to pull him out of there and dust him off. "Really, Dad, I am serious, what were you thinking?"

It was funny until I was bawling graveside, dodging people jogging through the cemetery.

Visiting the grave was like a wild card—I had no idea what emotions I would experience.

On a third trip, I went with my mother. We collected stones and brought them to my father's gravesite and stood there, side by side, awkward with one another. I wanted silence; she wanted to talk. We said something nice. We tried. Her way, my way, so different. But we tried.

Graveyard visits are important, complex, unexpected, fraught, comforting—all of the all. They can bring peace or cause total storms of emotional subterfuge.

Do it your way, on your clock, when you are ready. In six days, or in six years.

It's your grief. It's your loss. It's your life. Paying homage, being with the grave—or whatever your marker may be, wherever, however—it can help with coming to terms with the reality of this very hard to digest truth.

At one full year, I flew to be with my family for the gravestone unveiling ceremony. This marker, this movement from the nebulous to the concrete. *Kaddish* was long over, now was time to seal the year of mourning.

Early, hours before the ceremony, I snuck to the cemetery and expecting that same vacant gravesite, I was shocked to find the ornate headstone already there. It was glorious, beautifully etched with a photograph my father took of a clock, and a Hebrew quote that translates to "Justice, Justice, ye shall pursue." It felt like someone had dressed my dead father in a gorgeous tuxedo. I was so pleased, so happy he wasn't naked in the ground with no marker.

Up to this point, his grave, according to Jewish ritual tradition, remained an unmarked patch of dirt. The comfort the headstone brought me helped me to understand the profundity of an unveiling ceremony.

I felt my father's life was honored, and, because of this, it was easier for me to accept his being buried.

We had a ceremony as a family after that. The formal unveiling was a ten-person gathering by the grave. This time I remembered to wear appropriate shoes. The head-stone was now covered, cloaked, something to be ceremoniously revealed to all except for sneaky me. My sister flew in with her wife and two kids, joining my brother and his wife; my mother; the rabbi and her husband; and four family friends that are like family; plus, on Zoom, my father's brother in California.

My father was again dignified. The whole thing was sweet and also absurd. The kids were running loose through the cemetery, ripping stones off graves and throwing them everywhere as their moms attempted to find and replace the stones—Jewish ritual objects of love and prayer and care in lieu of what might elsewhere be flowers. My brother had a selfie stick and a tripod, and we were getting my uncle a good view for the iPhone Zoom call.

I had such a deep and sacred time alone at the grave that I felt irritated at the cer-emony. It was sad, it was collective, it reminded me of his funeral and burial—over-whelming in the memories it brought up—and this time the sentiments spoken were not my own. So many feelings. I wanted to run from the cemetery again. I wanted to go eat pancakes or go swimming or shopping—I wanted to get the fuck out of there.

But this was also healing, also us together, also bringing up all the buried pieces of me I was trying so hard to control. Bad and good. Both were important to me, collec-tive and individual rituals, different and vital. I felt changed afterwards, like this ritual had, in fact, closed my year of mourning. And something in me felt stronger than ever; being single wasn't even on my radar. Alone, I was finding so much meaning, so much sacredness, so much support from deep inside of me.

Whether it is a cremation and the tossing of ashes to the sea, a formal wake, or any number of other traditions—do the formal laying-to-rest your way. Every tradition has their way—stones, ashes, land, sea, nothing, everything. For me, the physical markers, the ways to see that my father's life could be visited, marked, this mattered to me.

And then, mark one year—your way—a year from the day of death or a year from the day of burial or a year from your last hug—a year or whatever measurement of time you love, Wiccan and beyond, just choose a day to mark a transition from the time inside the sacred year of mourning, and then, to stepping outside of it. Mark a pivot for your own personal transformation.

These markers do not mean that mourning has ended.

It does not mean you won't have pangs of loss, won't yearn for the deceased, it just means you are marking a time of transition, the possibility of a slow and gentle movement toward rejoining the living. It won't happen all at once, but these tools of closure make it much easier to integrate an understanding of the loss into the fabric of our days.

Eventually, when I went back to New Orleans, I did feel different. I felt less struck down with horrifying shock, less confusion when I remembered my dad. The slow realization that he was dead and gone was making its way into my consciousness. I found myself with more space, less panic, and I was more easily engaged in joyful activity. I was no longer in the era of what-the-fuck-happened-to-my-father-and-my-life. Now I was in the era of this-is-the-new-normal.

Was my grief "complete"?

Was I done when I did not fall over crying anymore, did not pass out spontaneously? No. I was still grieving, even after I re-regulated my nervous system. Is grief completion the completion of the trauma, when symptoms of distress cease? Many a shrink will mark "healthy" as able to work. Many will mark "complete" when the trauma symptoms subside.

I do not believe in rules that bind the practice of grieving to a finite map, a binary of right or wrong. I wondered so many times if I was grieving wrong. My maps, for grief and everything else, require on repeat that I pave a new path for myself, that I decide what is the "proper" way for me as an individual. No British house mother here in New Orleans telling me how much sad is *too much sad*. It's between me, myself, and I, and the things I want from this life.

And your grief is yours.

I am not angry, not this week. I am not haunted, not this week. I might be tomorrow. I still have bouts of anger, they return in waves when I long for my father and feel powerless that I can't bring him back. I still, sometimes, want to punch walls when I realize I will never see my dad again.

One thing is for certain: I will never again feel like I felt when my father was alive. But it was at this part of the process I was ready to step forward into my future, even if that meant without my dad. As my mother always says, where one branch breaks, another grows in its place.

We are, in this process of grieving, reborn within ourselves—part of us forever missing as new parts emerge.

HOW TO *BE* THE GRIEF SUPPORT

When it became my turn to be the support to others, after my year of deep loss, I employed every tool I possibly could from all I learned in the year before. Here's a review:

- **Honor your boundaries and be realistic about where you are at.** If you are mourning deeply one day, and someone asks you to be their grief support, nicely say, "no." No is better than drama. No is better than an explosion. No is love. Always when saying no to a griever, offer an alternate option. "I want to be there for you, but sadly I can't today. Does next Tuesday work?" They don't need too much info, just a sign that you are there, that you love them, that they aren't alone in this blustery world.

- **Listen.** Meditate or tend to yourself so deeply before you head over, knowing this time will not be about you, but solely about them. The deepest medicine to a grieving person is presence, unabated connection. Offer this. Be still inside so you can take their stories in. Remember that death and loss and trauma interrupt connection. Human care is medicine only when it is present to the possibilities of connection in this very present moment. Got the memo? Presence.

- **Do not project.** This is not connection. This is narcissism. Instead of presuming to know their experience, or overlaying your own on theirs, let them tell you. Let them lead you. And take their cues. They might be prickly, moody, difficult—this is not about you. Be gentle. They are in so much pain.

- It's okay to ask little things, like "Would you like to speak about what happened?" Or, "Would it be helpful to have a distraction? I can talk to you about gossip instead?" But don't push without first checking their limits. **Ask before asking, if that makes sense.** "How did they die?" is not a great thing to say. "Do you want to talk about the death?" This is the gentle way. Don't force them into memory they are not ready for. Let them choose the landscape of memory and conversation.

- **Bring tangible offerings.** Things that die, like flowers, depending on a person's traditional background, can be a burden right after death. Food is nice, candles are nice, blankets and slippers and body oils and the like, comforting objects—trust yourself. Don't show up empty-handed, though. I was grateful for every single offering. Especially ones that came from the heart.

- **If you want to pray, ask, "Is prayer something comforting and comfortable for you?"** If you want to talk about the afterlife, make it a discussion only when the griever leads. This, again, is not a time about you, about your beliefs, about what comforts you. It is about making yourself an offering, a vessel for the person you care for. If you have prayer to offer, let them choose it. But don't force things.

- **Ask before you touch.** Often a grieving person is also traumatized by any number of things. Do not reach in for the bear hug without first pausing, looking them in the eye, and asking directly, "Would it be okay to offer you a hug?" I don't care if this interruption to your flow makes you uncomfortable. It's not about you. The last thing you want to do is trigger and disturb the person you are trying to comfort. If they say no, don't comment. Don't push it. Let them lead you.

- I can't stress enough the vital importance of **taking care of you, of nurturing yourself before and during and after visiting with a griever.** Be quiet. Be still. Leave your fears at home. Process them with a friend before the visit. It's okay to cry, to be real, and to be honest, but from the rawness of the moment, not from the wells of neurosis bottled within. Grief rips veils. In these moments, being a raw beautiful human with the other raw beautiful human, on their terms, is best.

- **Remember: Everything, when you enter that room, is on their terms.** Think like you are visiting royalty. It is their way. It is their needs. Their limits to conversations. They are suffering. You are not there for you. You are there for them. If you are dealing with a hell of your own, deal with it before you get to this person's home. And only bring it up if they explicitly ask. Hearing your pain might be comforting to them. But only if solicited. They very well may have zero percent capacity to hear about hard or bad things. You can't know. Let. Them. Lead. You. And go home and get nourished elsewhere. Don't be angry if they aren't making space for you. That's not okay. They are at empty. Expect nothing. Lead with the positive, the gentle, the kind.

- **Don't force positive thinking on a griever.** Don't say, "Well at least . . ." Show up with light. Show up ready to take them in, to give them love. But do not force them to think about a fantastical idea of "good" when they are rubbing up against the truth of the grave.

- And if you don't go to the funeral, or the shiva, or hold their hand over tea, if it's too much for you, again, that's okay. Knowing that in advance is really wonderful. **They have other friends, other lovers, other family, other support.** Send food, a card, a gift, something, for their sake and for yours. And even if you are certain they don't have anyone but you, you can, from a distance, love a person deeply in times of mourning while still honoring your own boundaries and needs.

- **When you know you can't handle their loss, don't disappear.** Don't ghost them. Ghosting sucks for people who are already haunted. Never ignore the messages of someone in mourning. Ever. But again, do send them a package, a note, a meal, an emissary of another friend who is ready, who is able, who can handle this raw moment even if you can't.

- **Be honest.** Grievers are wise oracles. Just remember: it is not about you right now. It is about them, but make your choices in offering care in a way that also considers your own boundaries. Let how you show up honor your own set of protective parameters. And in whatever way and whatever capacity you choose to show up, again, make it 100 percent about them.

CHAPTER 13

LIFE AFTER DEATH: FINDING JOY

"IF I BAKE YOU A CAKE WILL IT HELP YOU FORGET?"

—J.S. Ondara, *Tales of Isolation* ("Mr. Landlord")

"I WANT YOU TO KNOW THAT RADICAL JOY DOES NOT MEAN BEING HAPPY ALL OF THE TIME, IT MEANS UNDERSTANDING THAT THERE IS PAIN AND INVESTING WHATEVER WE CAN INTO JOY AMIDST THAT."

—Vivi Nguyen, Owner, Radical Joy Bakery, New Orleans, LA

When Christmas subsides in New Orleans, and the trees are dragged out into the street, the lights stay up. New Year's marks the transition to another holiday season. The float building, the costume design, the meticulous beading for the Wild Tchoupitoulas, Bayou Renegades, and other Mardi Gras Indian Tribes, the ornate beaning for the Krewe of Red Beans parade, the gilding of shoes and coconuts for coveted Muses and Zulu tosses—often a full year of work comes to fruition.

By January 6, the Joan of Arc parade begins the season, and for the weeks to follow, long before the arrival of Fat Tuesday in all its glory, New Orleans courts parade after parade: local parades, dance team parades, artist parades, protest parades, goddess parades—all preludes to the big money parades of Endymion and beyond.

This time, I was ready.

By February, thirteen months since my father died, my second Mardi Gras, I was a regular on the block. I yelled exuberantly across porches, I knew the neighbors' trucks, dogs, children, and grandchildren, understood when to move my car to avoid street flooding, and how to pull beads and other debris from the drains to prevent the over-flow of water. I knew about potholes the size of whole cars, and I knew about fixing rotting wood before Mother's Day, the onset of flying termite season. I was close with my Terminix on call pest controller.

My knee was mostly healed.

My house was now a home, an homage to all my father had dreamed of for me, and the walls were covered with masks, crowns, a single precious Muses shoe gifted to me by a sacred Muses neighbor, and other costume pieces from masquerade after masquerade. I knew where the community gardens were. I knew how to get a CSA with locally farmed sweet potatoes, pecans, satsuma oranges, Ponchatoula strawberries, and cabbage twice the size of my own head. I enjoyed sunset at the lakefront, Saturdays alone by the water in Bay St. Louis, slow Sundays on my front porch with friends. I was home. I had mapped my life in this new city, including where to buy groceries, and where to get a pap smear. I knew the secret to getting the cheapest gas in town.

Here, in New Orleans, so much more is breathing. The dead are buried above ground. The city is below sea level, salt is in the air. My father maybe knew, as he helped me land here, that he was preparing me for the year to come, for losing him, for a year of mourning, for beginning the rest of my life. Here in this place where so many come to grieve, and to celebrate. This place where we are asked to come alive, to burst forth in joy, the twin to loss.

And just like I adjusted to New Orleans, learned when lizard season came and went, mosquito season, allergy season, and navigated leaving my old life, so, too, was I able to navigate the difficult discombobulating terrain of my grief, of the aftermath of my father's death. Somehow now, in the season of costumes and tosses and festivals and cake, in the midst of a city-wide party, I had found my new normal. My grief was not gone, by any means, but it was as if, once again, I had found my feet.

It took a year to unveil some semblance of what a new normal might look like.

My Mid-City block was once shrouded in darkness—no electricity for months on end, at least four feet of water in the homes, debris, mold, and a total lack of infrastructure everywhere. And in Flood Zone X, my block, though in some places under ten feet of water, was a lucky block—a spared block.

Nearby, when buying a fried catfish Po-Boy (not kosher, I know) at Katie's on Iberville, I always make note of a subtle plaque by the front door reading: "Water Line: Katrina 2005." The plaque is at roughly seven feet. Mandina's up the street,

Finn McCool's, and so many other neighborhood restaurants and bars are resurrections from the debris. So many businesses, houses, street poles and signs, schools and churches in this neighborhood had to navigate being stripped of everything. And then, so many returned.

There are scars. Don't forget the scars remain. Permanent scars, lives lost, displaced, ruined.

This city, where I have made a home but will always be a guest on sacred Chitimacha land, this house, these 100-year-old flood-surviving wooden floors, I bow to. I am in awe of this place. I am in awe of the will to survive, the way cultural practices live on—how Second Lines and Mardi Gras Indians and everything on Claiborne and beyond continues with fervor. There is a reason why people come here when they need to remember their vitality. This is New Orleans, an emblem of strength and perseverance.

If New Orleans, the most miraculous, resilient, and remarkable city on earth could keep its joy, magnify its joy, share its joy, bring others to joy, then so can you.

I have a hunch you will find your new normal.

Every time.

And that this new normal will be nothing like the last one.

It took me a year to truly recover my joy. For some it takes much longer. For others joy is the one thing gripped, never lost sight of, a medicine vital in times of loss. Throughout the mourning process joy, a light. Joy—leaping, dancing, unbridled letting go—this took time for me. It did not return all at once. Joy hurt at first. Every new thing reminded me that my dad wasn't here to see, to enjoy, to talk it out, to celebrate with me. Every new thing showed me just how gone he was, that my dad was still supercalifragilistically dead. Every new thing made me feel alive, and subsequently, more aware that he was not.

Happiness sold as perpetual sunshine is a marketing scheme. It lives in relationship to grief, in relationship to sadness; it mandates a balance. Your happiness will not be perpetual. It will come in waves, and it will subside. But flexing the muscle of enjoying your life, when possible, is a practice. My grief, it was not gone—my dad lived in the seams. My sadness over losing him still came in waves, but things were different now.

New Orleans taught me how to leave the paradigm of expectation, to step away from defining myself by a diamond ring and marriage, and instead, to define myself by how good a time I can muster, share—how to make love a practice of sharing communal joy. A joy that everyone, I mean everyone, should have access to.

And, my joy was deeper now. I grew louder when I laughed. And while I once took them for granted, now the feelings of happiness struck me like a gentle wave passing through every cell of my body. I was highly attuned to good feelings, after so many bad ones. I became so deeply grateful for my life.

I was ready, in the words of the great Akilah Oliver, to "walk the carnival."

On All King's Day, Savanah and I drive to Bywater Bakery and get a freshly baked Chantilly cream and berries king cake. We sit in the car in silence in the middle of the afternoon. We eat cake for lunch. Slowly, with our eyes closed.

It is that good.

It is the time for joy.

The blood has returned.

My grief, not gone, perhaps never gone, but lessened. It is the time to relish life, to drive with the windows down and shout to people in the streets with an outpouring of love. It is time for the craft table to move to the living room, to get out the hot glue gun, to cut up the clothes that no longer fit after this year of eating and crying and mending, and to rework them into magisterial costume attire.

Here, in New Orleans, we dance, we eat cake in groups, we gild our bodies like royalty, we ride through the streets and beg everyone in our path to come alive.

Here, we celebrate the fact that we are so lucky to be so deeply alive.

Death does not kill joy. Disaster does not kill joy.

Joy is a birthright.

By the time Valentine's Day rolls around, romance and coupledom are forgotten in pursuit of communal dance, communal costumes, communal presents, communal drinking, eating, wandering, and witnessing a community engaging in fantasy together, on every street corner, in every inch of the city.

So, we ride.

On a Saturday afternoon I don something old: my grandmother's hot pink scarf. Something new: a glittered Pegasus crown. Something borrowed: my friend Abby's red tutu. And something blue: my father's button-down shirt. This is a fête of massive proportion—double, triple, really 100 times the size of any wedding I have ever attended.

And everyone, I mean everyone, is invited.

I join my krewe, a blinged-out, glitzed-up group of utopian apocalyptic warrior people. There are unicorns and there are octopus legs, soldiers of love from the future, and women in unitards that sparkle for what feels like miles. Everyone in tights and wigs, genders dissolve, everyone has lights in their hair, and the bicycles are blinking, are pouring over with flowers, with wings and propellers.

We are the future.

Single? Lonely? Please. We are eating cake and riding hard.

And, in the spirit of New Orleans, a borrowed method, we ride through the city inviting anyone willing to witness our joy to participate. There are no limits to this one. "Express Yourself" is blasting. People rush to their porches. This is like finding the ice cream man on your block, times ten. This is contagious communal joy. Better than sex. Just a group of adults remembering to play, remembering to enjoy the delight of personal transformation, putting their creativity on full peacock display for all to relish. This is a group of adults dosing a city in joy.

People rush outside and scream, "Happy Mardi Gras!" Everyone wants in. Everyone wants a release. Children leap and run beside us like puppies. It's safe. It's at a distance. It's gentle and yet loud.

And there are prizes.

The Krewe of Goddesses will parade and hand out the delicacies of gilded oyster shells. The Krewe of Muses emerge, their shoes decked out. It's an endless unfolding, as if everyone in one single place wants to remind you that you aren't alone, that you can join the fray, that collectively we have this acute capacity for a good time. It's a kid's birthday party times one thousand, and everyone leaves with beads, with goodies, with prizes and smiles.

And there's cake.

Did I mention the cake?

There is so much cake.

Praline. Chantilly cream. Frangipane. Cream cheese frosted. Goat cheese and apple, cream cheese and cinnamon. Radical Joy's Funfetti cake. Randazzo's traditional. There's King Cake Pop-Tarts®, Saba's babka king cake, Mangazzo's, Gambino's, Brennan's pink parade strawberry cream cheese. There's the "Elvis" from La Boulangerie, with peanut butter, banana, toasted chocolate marshmallows, and bacon, walnut frangipane with apple cider vinegar glaze and cream cheese frosting from Bayou St. Cake, azul dulce blueberry from Bywater Bakery, *galette des rois* from Bearcat, and the favorite, Dong Phuong's strawberry from New Orleans East.

I had wailed. I had beaten my chest. I had torn at my hair and tossed myself towards the grave. I mourned. I was the bereaved. I grieved. I lamented. I lay down, flat, kissing the earth. And, as is the way, joy did, in fact, return.

My father did not.

They who sow in tears shall reap with songs of joy.

I grew up hearing the expression "never forget." My father even wrote it as an epitaph to a seventh-grade research paper. It is about remembering the horror of what happened to our family, and, I will add, maybe yours.

Rabbi Simcha Zissel Ziv, a nineteenth century Mussar Rabbi says, "Remembering death in the proper way can bring a person to the ultimate joy." My additional caveat to the family mantra, after all these years of learning, comes from the *Chassidic* mystical worship of delight: never forget joy. Never forget that the pain you feel in mourning is in part because of how deeply you loved someone, something, some time, some state of being. Celebrate that love. Never forget it.

And then, dance.

ACKNOWLEDGMENTS

In gratitude to those who have held me this year, in sickness and in health. To my mother, first and foremost. For your strength and love and patience and amazing mind. To my sister, Daniela, and my brother, David, and to Liv and Talia and Alma and Aviv for being the lights in this weird tunnel. And for holding me through the process of reliving my grief to write this book. To my teachers. To Reb Nadya and Reb Shefa, to Bhanu and Stefania, Joelle and Naomi and Deena and Selah and Nancy. To Robert and James and Reed, and to Rabbis Meir, Cooper, Broitman, Alexander, Goldberg, Ingber, and the many others who taught me about all I contain. To the late and great Akilah. To all of you who taught me to write, and to grieve.

In gratitude to the great city of New Orleans. In gratitude to Mandala Earth and Insight Editions.

To my brave therapists, I know it wasn't easy. To my healers, especially Ty, Nancy, Andrea, Thuy, and Melissa.

And to the many other people who held me in my grief: Jessica, Ilse, Mara, Nina, Tammy and Eda, Eva, Sol, Sam, Shelley, Ruthie and all the cousins, and to Noah, Daniel, Ndidi, Jon, Oliver, Molly, Jefferson, Emily, Camille, Sarah, Jenn, Zada, Kiese, and so many others who tended to my broken heart. And to those who held me, and shaped my life in New Orleans: Kat, Savanah, Josh, Gilad, Eliza, Katherine, Naomi, Annie, Virginia, Charlie, Julia, Jim, Arthur, Poppy, Alon, Emily, Michelle, Christine, Jerome, and all the rest. And to my readers and project advisors, especially Giulia, Sam, and Matt. And also to Katherine, to Audrey, to Zada, to Eryn, to Tim and Lexie and Emily and Jefferson, to Mara, to Jake, to Susie, to Abby, to Sruly, to Ping, to Irene, to Eliza, to David, to Rachel, to Tannaz, to Salem, to Nicki, to Michelle, to Kim, to Caroline, to Ndidi, to Deva, to Shana, to Deb, and of course, to the great Chlöe Berlin.

It is all of you I will cherish, from this day forward, until death do us part.

In gratitude to Naropa. In gratitude to the Graduate Theological Union. In gratitude to Pardes. In gratitude to Sivananda. In gratitude to Kohenet. In gratitude to Aleph. In gratitude to all the other institutions that taught me how important it is to reduce suffering in myself first, and then the world. For teaching me how to live.

May all beings find ease in their grief.

In gratitude, most of all, to my father, Allan Gerson, may his memory always be for a blessing.

MANDALA

An imprint of MandalaEarth
PO Box 3088 San Rafael, CA 94912
www.MandalaEarth.com

Find us on Facebook: www.Facebook.com/MandalaEarth
Follow us on Twitter: @MandalaEarth

PUBLISHER: Raoul Goff

ASSOCIATE PUBLISHER: Phillip Jones

CREATIVE DIRECTOR: Chrissy Kwasnik

ASSOCIATE ART DIRECTOR: Ashley Quackenbush

DESIGN SUPPORT: Mallory Price

EDITORIAL DIRECTOR: Katie Killebrew

MANAGING EDITOR: Matt Wise

EDITORIAL ASSISTANT: Sophia Wright

SENIOR PRODUCTION MANAGER: Greg Steffen

ROOTS of PEACE   REPLANTED PAPER

Earth Aware Editions, in association with Roots of Peace, will plant two trees for each tree used in the manufacturing of this book. Roots of Peace is an internationally renowned humanitarian organization dedicated to eradicating land mines worldwide and converting war-torn lands into productive farms and wildlife habitats. Roots of Peace will plant two million fruit and nut trees in Afghanistan and provide farmers there with the skills and support necessary for sustainable land use.

Manufactured in Turkey by Insight Editions

10 9 8 7 6 5 4 3 2